Dick

Change is the only constant in life. My very best as you enter the next phase of your career. It no doubt will be challenging and exciting.

Warm regards

Rose Kennedy
1996

D1314038

The Orders of Change

Building Value-Driven Organizations

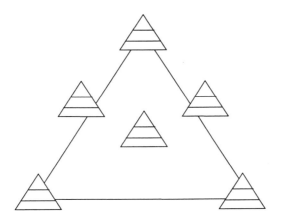

Rose L. Kennedy
Edited by Richard H. Greb

McGraw-Hill, Inc.
College Custom Series

New York St. Louis San Francisco Auckland Bogotá
Caracas Lisbon London Madrid Mexico Milan Montreal
New Delhi Paris San Juan Singapore Sydney Tokyo Toronto

The Orders of Change
Building Value-Driven Organizations

1a 2 3 4 5 6 7 8 9 DOC/DOC 9 9 8 7 6 5

ISBN 0-07-034081-1
Editor: Reaney Dorsey
Printer/Binder: R. R. Donnelly & Sons Company

TABLE OF CONTENTS

PART II
A Case Study of the *Hospital of the Future* Project

Preface

This book examines the three Orders of Change and the ability of the organization to deal in these three areas to effect organizational transformation. It illustrates the application of the three Orders of Change with the development of the Irvine Medical Center (IMC) in Irvine, California.

The book is a snapshot in time. My goal is to demonstrate how the three Orders of Change were used in the design of IMC. This book looks at the project from IMC's construction to the opening of the hospital (1986–1990)—and the lessons learned—not to assess responsibility for success or failure. The important thing is the way the three Orders of Change came together and the lessons this teaches about reinventing organizations. I have made no effort to revisit IMC to see what has happened since the project ended. And in fact, its parent company, American Medical International, Inc. (AMI), no longer exits in the same form. Ownership and control of the organization have changed hands, and comments relating to AMI reflect the way it existed at the time.

The insights drawn from the building of this one hospital offer insights for any organization seeking to reinvent itself and create a future in which external economics and internal organizational values are aligned, to the benefit of all their stakeholders.

Never, before nor since, to this author's knowledge, has any effort of this magnitude been tried in the health care industry. IMC was a hospital under construction. Even as its physical foundation was being laid, so was the cultural construct in which it was ultimately to operate. The challenge was to create a *Hospital of the Future*, breaking paradigms, destroying sacred cows and daring to be different in ways that would add shareholder value, and deliver excellence in patient care.

Causing change to happen requires an enormous amount of courage and stamina. It is not for the faint of heart. When this project began in 1986, the idea of constant change was just beginning to be recognized. Joel Barker had not yet introduced the business world to Thomas Kuhn and paradigm thinking. Charles Handy had not yet brought home the realization that the "age of unreason" was upon us; that, to move into the 21st Century, we would have to abandon old ways of thinking about change; that the new change required was discontinuous from what had gone before, and that organizations needed to start change with a blank sheet of paper. Jack Welch at General Electric had not yet demonstrated that self-directed work teams can and do generate growth and profit for an organization, and Gary Hamel's concept that future organizations must move from re-engineering to reinventing in order to compete was not part of the business lexicon.

However, these ideas were taking shape in one tiny corner of southern California. A small band of revolutionaries was using its combined knowledge and experience to challenge and re-challenge each other's hypotheses of how hospitals work. It drew on concepts that I introduced to other AMI hospitals in the United States and England, and their best practices Charged with examining whether or not a hospital can be transformed, the group dismantled and examined every component of patient care delivery. The project was stimulating and exciting, an opportunity to actually create something new and different as a template for a better future.

This change project left its imprint on everyone. It is difficult to explain fully the dedication that went with its creation. Lives were literally put on hold; personal decisions such as when to have a child were factored against when the hospital would actually open its doors. Seven-day work schedules were the norm. The vision of a hospital of the future became all-consuming. Everyone connected to the project felt its impact. The atmosphere was highly charged; excitement permeated the air. As new people joined, they felt the contagion and commitment. We were raising the bar for health care delivery with an organizational design that was value driven. People were expected to model daily the values that became the cornerstones of IMC.

To those IMC revolutionaries: the individuals who were willing to open their minds to possibilities, who made personal sacrifices and who helped make their collective vision a reality, I say thank you; thank you for inviting me to be a part of the revolution. In particular, I want to recognize John C. Gaffney, IMC's CEO, for his courage and persistent leadership; Susan (Karch) Murphy, for her passion for people and her desire toward service excellence; Jan Kerchner, for selecting quality physicians who wanted a different kind of facility in which to practice; Ericka Waidley, who found a place for her creative patient case management approach; Gail Stearns, whose role as executive assistant to the team was invaluable; and David Spector and George

MacEarchern, who had the thankless job of trying to explain the financial systems and new technologies of this extraordinary hospital to the parent company.

I offer a special acknowledgment to Gene E. Burleson and the late Robert C. Bohlman, who, during their tenures at AMI, Inc., recognized and challenged fundamental change in the delivery of health care.

My thanks also to my dogged editor and friend, Richard H. Greb, without whom my notes would have remained scattered, and to Becky Strehlow who helped us refine the manuscript. Most importantly, I am indebted to the revolutionary in my life, my son, Michael J. Kennedy, whose ongoing support, encouragement (as well as constant nagging) and trust in my abilities brought this book to its completion.

Rose L. Kennedy — February 1995

Introduction

All change involves some resistance. Even when the change is viewed as a positive one, it is a jolt to the system both organizationally and individually. Change means a shift from the known to the unknown and, even if the known has been unpleasant, people have adjusted and are able to cope with it. . . . People reluctantly give up familiar places, habits and routines.
—Traveling through White Water:
A Manager's Guide for Organizational Change

For organizations to succeed, they must recognize that their environment will change continually and that they must learn to anticipate change and set about managing it in an organized way. They must map out what they want to be different and define the capabilities, skills, attitudes, responsibilities and accountabilities that will lead their people to those outcomes. Moreover, they must give their people a reality that matches their words. Organizations must do more than just "talk the talk."

There must be a demonstrated commitment to the change process because fundamental change-that which is embodied in a new culture-does not happen in the space of a few months. It sometimes takes years before a fundamental change becomes institutionalized.

Managing fundamental change effectively enhances the long-term growth of the organization and positions it to capitalize on new business opportunities. It cuts down the time managers and employees spend resisting change, reducing the problems and costs of lost business that can accompany forced change or failure to change. Fundamental change is not "business as usual." It requires that the organization develop both a change plan *and* an implementation plan. At the core of these plans are the values the organization has identified as vital to reinventing itself.

An organization cannot change effectively without a set of values and guiding beliefs. This emphasis on values is essential because it transforms principles into practice.

Organizations traditionally spend little time analyzing whether or not the values set forth through vision and mission statements actually are aligned and being practiced. Phrases posted on walls throughout corporate America proclaiming "our customers come first" and " we are committed to customer service," do not, in themselves, make reality. The truth comes not from the stated values but from what actually occurs. If there is a choice between serving the customer immediately or completing paperwork first, the decision made reflects whether individuals are committed to and practice "customers come first." Aligning stated values with behavior is fundamental for organizations that want a competitive edge.

This penetration into the essence of the organization can be likened to an iceberg. The tip of the organization is First Order Change. Its components include the vision and mission of the organization, business strategies, and its stated organizational values. There are also goals and objectives, policies and procedures, structure, formal reward system as well as training and development.

Below the tip of the iceberg are Second and Third Order Change. Second Order Change encompasses the inherent behavioral aspects of the organization: individual values and beliefs, leadership styles, attitudes, motivations, communication patterns, individual self-esteem, working relationships and informal rewards.

Whereas First Order Change is quantitative, Second Order Change is qualitative and therefore more difficult to measure. It is, however, the only path an organization can take into Third Order Change and only in Third Order Change does fundamental organizational transformation take place. It is in the Third Order that individuals become accountable for practicing the organization's values; where there is a total system connectiveness to running the business, and where ongoing change is the order of the day.

Although only the tip of the iceberg is visible, its movements necessarily reflect those of the whole. So it is with the Orders of Change. All three must move in tandem.

One illustration of how the Orders of Change apply came in creating the *Hospital of the Future* in Irvine, California, for American Medical International, Inc. (AMI). A group of dedicated health care professionals, drawing on change projects successfully implemented at other AMI facilities, defined the processes necessary to implement the perfect hospital. Irvine Medical Center (IMC) was the first full-scale effort to make the *Hospital of the Future* a reality. It existed for a brief, shining moment, acknowledged as very special by those who experienced it, both internally and externally; but in the end, the inertia of the industry and a parent company that grew further from the hospital's goals and values over the course of the project, eroded the promise of a new future and returned Irvine to the ranks of the common.

Part I of this book outlines the Three Orders of Change along with the key processes used on this project to bridge the gap between theory and practice. Part II discusses the *Hospital of the Future* and the lessons learned from that project.

PART I

Theoretical Underpinnings of Change

If you always do
What you've always done
You'll always get
What you've always gotten.

–anonymous

Chapter 1. Orders of Change

Change is a Process, Not an Event

The idea of changing organizations is not new. Organizations are continually looking for ways to improve their performance. The pitfall is looking for the quick fix rather than recognizing that change is a multilayered process requiring management and long-term commitment. The time needed to make substantive changes is measured not in months but in years.

Ways to approach change abound. Since World War II, "fad" solutions have proliferated. A range of quick fix management theories were tried across the industrial world: Theory Z management, management by objectives, portfolio management, one-minute management, restructuring, computerization, management by walking around, intrapreneuring, zero-based budgeting, TQM and re-engineering, among others. Indeed, the concern is that, as the number of solutions is increasing, they are being shifted in—and out—of place at an ever accelerating rate.

There is nothing inherently wrong with any of these ideas. The problem is with executives who use them as bandages, not thinking through their impact on the total organization. Without sincere and full commitment from top management, and without the time to take hold, these methods are doomed to failure. Worse, they undermine morale, management loses credibility and the next effort at change is accompanied by management protestations that it is not just another fad, protestations that become more empty and less effective with each failed attempt.

One way to understand the dynamic of organizational change is to compare it to an iceberg *(Illustration 1)*. The tip of the iceberg, First Order Change, is where most change initiatives occur. First Order Change has merit since, by its very nature, it is attempting to enhance or improve the organization. For example, in recent years, it has become popular to streamline the structure of the organization by removing several managerial layers. Explanations accompanying the structural changes include such descriptors as "decision making at the point of service" or "empowering the workplace." When such restructuring is examined closely, however, it becomes evident that power has simply been consolidated in fewer managers. Another popular First Order Change

8

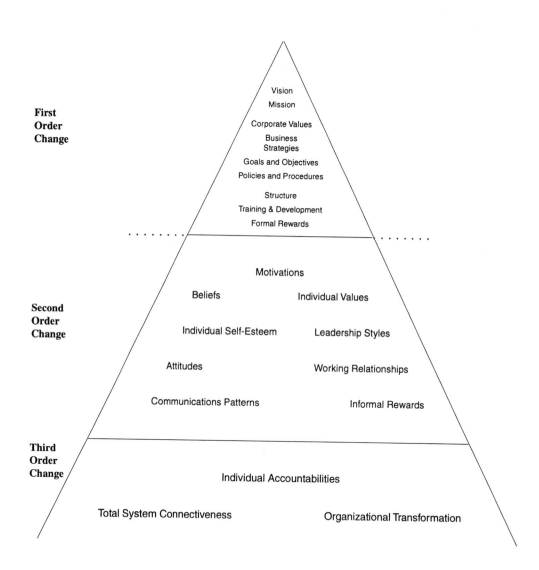

First Order Change

Vision
Mission
Corporate Values
Business Strategies
Goals and Objectives
Policies and Procedures
Structure
Training & Development
Formal Rewards

Second Order Change

Motivations
Beliefs
Individual Values
Individual Self-Esteem
Leadership Styles
Attitudes
Working Relationships
Communications Patterns
Informal Rewards

Third Order Change

Individual Accountabilities
Total System Connectiveness
Organizational Transformation

Illustration 1: The Orders of Change

promotes customer services, but merely talking of quality services and products can only go a limited distance. These First Order shifts do not penetrate below the surface to Second Order Change.

The organization that intends to make fundamental change to cope with an ever-moving complex business environment will not succeed until the stated new values (First Order) match the actions and individual values (Second Order Change). These values and beliefs must be absorbed and modeled by the individuals responsible for implementing them. Talk can only go a limited distance unless managers think systemically. They must recognize the links among First and Second Order Change components in the organization and that the organization needs to align everyday work practices with its principles. Note that individual values and beliefs make up the bulk of the iceberg in Illustration 1. As with its physical counterpart, the bulk of organizational change is not readily visible but supports — and in fact moves — the tip of the iceberg.

People's behavior is based in their values. Values are beliefs that guide actions. An organization reinforces a system of collective beliefs that tell people what is "good" and what is "bad"; what is "acceptable" and "unacceptable" within that organization. These collective values have a strong effect on the performance of both individuals and the overall organization. People whose personal values are skew to the organization are uncomfortable and likely either to try to undermine the organization by challenging those values or, eventually, to leave the organization. The worst scenario is that these individuals stay and, because the organization is not holding them accountable for modeling the values, weaken the fabric of the organization. Over time, the organization continues to exist but is never able to excel.

To be effective, the organization must move to Second Order Change. It must make the underlying philosophies match and reinforce First Order Change in its efforts to achieve a true transformation, or Third Order Change. It must make the walk match the talk.

Third Order Change, where true paradigm shifts occur, allows an organization to break with the past and construct a new future. Third Order Change is the ultimate goal in transforming an organization and its culture. It is the lasting, non-revertible condition that will make the organization's stated values and beliefs as natural and consistent as breathing.

Dealing with Second and Third Order Change requires challenging the basic behaviors and attitudes of individuals. It means going beyond an individual's assumptions, attitudes and feelings to the very core of the values and beliefs that drive that individual. This explains why some individuals are incapable of accepting the organization's fundamental change, much less modeling the new values. An organization cannot make fundamental change without coming to an understanding of what values and beliefs it wants—and needs—to embrace and how these values and beliefs are reflected in its people.

First Order Change processes set out the framework in which the organization operates. It causes people to reexamine whether their values and behaviors are consistent with those of the organization.

Mere compliance with First Order Change forms a shaky foundation to successful fundamental change. It allows for inconsistent behaviors and inhibits true transformation. Changes are at best incremental and sporadic rather than substantive and permanent. This is not to say that First Order Change is insignificant. Organizations can—and do—exist in that state, but First Order Change alone results in a compliant, risk-averse environment. Organizations muddle along and are unable to make the bold changes necessary in today's "permanent white water"[1] to capture the competitive advantage of change. A gap forms between the organization and its people in which lie stresses that tend to push the organization back to its pre-change condition and stiffen resistance to future efforts at change.

Until all three Orders of Change are aligned, change is limited. To obtain flexibility, fluidity and longevity requires working on all three levels. Managing such fundamental change is a process that extends beyond the next quarterly or annual report, though the time taken to achieve significant change can be accelerated with thoughtful planning.

The Role of Culture

Effecting Second Order Change in an organization begins with an examination of its culture which is where the organization's shared beliefs and values lie. It is the culture that tells the organization's members what the organization stands for and, ultimately, the culture is the yardstick by which the organization's employees, shareholders, customers, regulators and the public at large judge it. As Stan Davis maintains in *Managing Corporate Culture* that beliefs fall into two categories, guiding beliefs and daily beliefs.[2]

These beliefs are linked with the Orders of Change. Guiding beliefs are First Order: the principles on which organizational strategies are based. Daily beliefs are Second Order, determining if strategies are realized. Guiding beliefs determine the organization's vision; daily beliefs make the vision a reality. The two categories must match if an organization is to grow successfully. It is useless to declare "customers are our most important value" or "quality is more important than rushing product out the door" unless every individual within the organization behaves in a way that reflects that in daily practices.

Daily beliefs are the basis for the ways that work is actually performed and the products or services delivered. They are below the water line in Second Order Change, and can only be felt when the organization's guiding beliefs and daily beliefs are aligned.

When a culture is healthy, the daily beliefs flow from the guiding beliefs; they are in harmony. The more unlinked the beliefs are to daily work, the more unlikely the organization will achieve Third Order Change.

Changing Behaviors

Organizations can mandate what they want when it comes to acceptable behavior; they cannot mandate values. When an organization sets out to make fundamental change, it is redefining its values. This distinction between behaviors and values is a significant consideration. The three Orders of Change are always in motion. On the surface, individuals may comply with the desired new organizational behaviors but below the surface, they may or may not place a high value on those behaviors. This disconnect between behaviors and values weakens the organization's progress toward true transformation.

Morris Massey describes acceptance of a new value as driven by a "significant event or action." He says that since values are imprinted on us by the age of 10, changing values means abandoning or replacing old values. This only occurs if individuals view the new value as being more powerful for them personally.[3] Individuals change behavior before changing values.

Managing behavioral change needs to be part of the change implementation plan. The plan requires a developmental component that gives individuals skill and practice in the new desired behaviors. This emphasis on learning behaviors to match the organization's values is a key intervention to move into Second Order Change and must be powerful enough to cause individuals to abandon the old behaviors and replace them with new ones.

Because the organization is attempting to change collective behaviors, it also must build in reinforcement. Qualitative behaviors must be reflected in performance measurements. How serious the organization is about change will be reflected in how it manages individuals whose behaviors are not aligned with those of the organization. Does it lower its standards of behavior or deal aggressively with the mismatch.

Once there is individual commitment to the new collective behaviors, chances are greatly enhanced that individuals will assimilate those behaviors into their personal values.

Summary

• First Order Change consists of establishing organizational values; the Second Order consists of individual values and behaviors; and Third Order is organizational transformation that takes place when First and Second Orders are aligned.

• Organizations that attempt to change by merely focusing on First Order Change limit their results if organizational values and individual values are not aligned.

• The goal of fundamental change is the alignment of First and Second Order Change. Moving to this level allows an organization to gain a competitive advantage by fully embracing the opportunities presented by change.

• Organizations can mandate acceptable behaviors; they cannot mandate values.

Chapter 2. Moving to Second and Third Orders of Change

Effecting Second and Third Order Change requires paying attention to the informal dynamics of the organization. Once that fundamental system of linkages is understood, a well-defined learning process can be used to reinvent the organization.

The Foundation of Change: Systems Thinking

Systems thinking is a holistic approach to working in organizations, an understanding that all parts of the system are linked together. One such systems approach is Marvin Weisbord's Six Box Organizational Model that defines six internal organizational subsystems.[4] The *mission* (what business is the organization in?), the *structure* (how does work actually get done?), the *rewards* (how do people know they are doing a good job?), the *helping mechanisms* (what resources/ technologies exist that support the organization's work), *relationships* (how do people manage conflicts?) and *leadership* (how is everyone helping keep the subsystems in balance?).

These subsystems illustrate the linkages required of the organization.

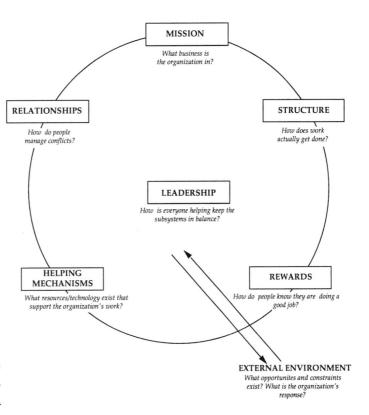

Illustration 2: Six Box Organizational Model

Complicating the internal interactions is the ongoing impact of the external environment. An organization is an open system and it adapts in a dynamic way. It cannot be static. The acknowledgment that change is continual means that a systems approach is imperative to organizational growth.

What an organization does both formally and informally is to continually scan its six subsystems to determine which, if any, are out of alignment due to forces, both from within and outside. If any are imbalanced, the organization needs to realign them, strengthening the weak subsystem which, if uncorrected, leads to decline in organizational performance.

Illustration 3: The Orders of Change and the Systems Model

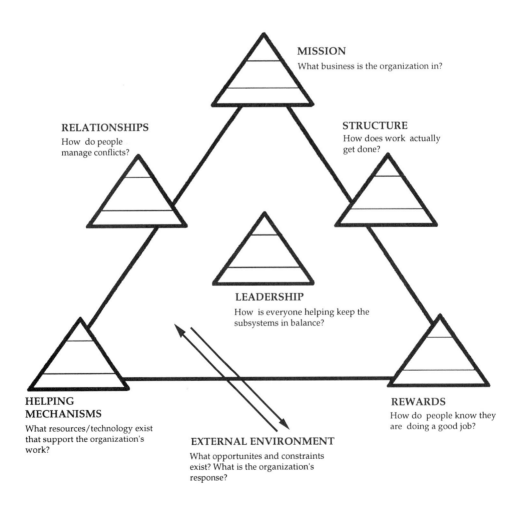

MISSION
What business is the organization in?

RELATIONSHIPS
How do people
manage conflicts?

STRUCTURE
How does work actually
get done?

LEADERSHIP
How is everyone helping keep the
subsystems in balance?

**HELPING
MECHANISMS**
What resources/technology exist
that support the organization's
work?

EXTERNAL ENVIRONMENT
What opportunites and constraints
exist? What is the organization's
response?

REWARDS
How do people know they
are doing a good job?

Because the environment is constantly changing, the organization must constantly respond, either by moving back to its internal equilibrium or by accommodating external forces. The most effective approach is anticipating the external direction and choosing to change the internal equilibrium before the organization becomes less and less effective in meeting its external competitive demands.

When an organization undertakes a cultural shift, it is altering all of its subsystems. Because each subsystem changes at its own rate, they will be out of alignment for a time and each must be managed. Concentrated efforts for each subsystem demands everyone be actively involved.

Superimposed onto each subsystem are the Three Orders of Change. For example, if the fundamental change is to redefine the business itself, the organization must determine its new corporate values (First Order); what new behaviors are required (Second Order); and how the whole system will be realigned (Third Order). Subsystems are in a dynamic equilibrium. Change in any one subsystems has implications for all the others. Measuring the organizational impact of change is crucial to planning successful change. Every subsystem and Order of Change needs to be examined to see that, as all shift, all still fit.

Alignment of the Organization's Subsystems

Organizations must design and tailor processes to support the change effort. When moving toward Third Order Change, they must pay attention to how each organizational subsystem will enhance or inhibit the ability of the organization to transform itself. The easier mechanisms are those that are quantifiable, e.g., a team compensation system. Qualitative mechanisms are more difficult to put in place, e.g., the behaviors required of a team compensation system.

Peter Senge describes the subsystems as "the invisible fabrics of inter-related actions which often take years to fully play out their effects on each other. Since we are part of that lacework ourselves, it is doubly hard to see the whole pattern of change. Instead, we tend to focus on snapshots of isolated parts of the system and wonder why our deepest problems never seem to get solved."[5]

Examining the total system connectiveness is a major challenge in itself. It requires organizations to consider the impact of change on all the stakeholders and, depending on the complexity of the change, to determine what is needed for each stakeholder to gain buy-in and commitment to the change. It means careful analysis of all the interrelated actions in each subsystem and whether they fit with the desired change. If not, someone needs to ascertain what needs to be done to address the gaps between the desired state and the current state.

The IMC project discussed addressed each subsystem and the three Orders of Change, with a heavy concentration on Second Order Change. It assessed fundamental behaviors and whether those behaviors matched the guiding values of the organization.

The key concepts IMC used to effect Second and Third Order Change included:

• Shared Leadership - a structure that leads to self-managed work teams and involves the whole work force.

• The Accountability Effect™ - an organizational principle that individual and team accountability build an empowered, effective work force.

• Value Hiring - a process that helps identify and hire individuals whose behaviors match the desired organizational values.

• Pay-for-Performance System - a reward system that aligns performance with the organization's values.

• Outcome Thinking® - an accountability model for a proactive approach to problem solving.

• Communication Integrity - a process that supports comprehensive, open, honest, relevant and fact-based communication contributing both internally and externally to overall organizational effectiveness.

• Experiential Learning - a training technology of learning by doing.

• Conflict and Working Relationships - a process that encourages individuals to use their differences to increase the organization's capacity for innovation and creativeness.

• Peer Review and Upward Management Review - performance reviews that encouragement ongoing feedback to individuals by their peers and subordinates, as well as to managers.

Shared Leadership

The intent of Shared Leadership is to foster an environment of self-management. Empowerment is the essence of Shared Leadership. People, for the most part, are self-reliant and will work for the good of their organizations when given the opportunity. Even beyond that, once they believe their views are important, they are willing to test new ideas and collectively work towards the betterment of the whole organization.

There are three key drivers to implementing Shared Leadership successfully:

1. *A full understanding of the organization's strategy.* Sharing the strategic plan with everyone in the organization helps increase indi vidual understanding and commitment to the plan.

2. *A full understanding of the organization's financial objectives.* When individuals understand the financial targets and the desired return on investment (ROI) they are more likely to feel accountable.

3. *A stake in the organization.* When people understand that they will gain, or lose, based on the ability of the *whole* organization to achieve its objectives, they will look for ways to collaborate more effectively.

Shared Leadership contains an interesting paradox. Somewhere, some-body has to begin the process. Leaders must say, "This is the way it's going to be." Then people either begin to match with the organization's values, or to leave because they do not embrace or believe in them. The empowered must be made accountable, which means leaders shape the working framework. But unless leaders value this way of working together, and act as role models for the organization, Second and Third Orders of Change will not happen. The resulting façade will, in fact, diminish the organization's credibility. Shared Leadership is designed to give individuals authority to make decisions at the point of service, making them responsible for the decisions that immediately affect their jobs and asking them to be active contributors to the organization's overall business decisions.

Implementation of a Shared Leadership approach requires a sophisticated hiring process selecting individuals who are willing to accept accountability for their actions.

Six beliefs underlie the Shared Leadership philosophy:

1. People can achieve their full potential and will work hard to do so.

2. People are honest and trustworthy; they want and deserve to be treated with respect and dignity.

3. Individuals in an organization learn from each other.

4. Individuals in an organization can identify and correct mistakes and problems before they escalate or are shifted to higher levels of the organization.

5. Individuals in an organization have an accountability and are responsible for the financial well-being of the organization.

6. There is no such thing as an information monopoly.

The Accountability Effect™

An organization is filled with leaders when people feel empowered to make decisions at the point of service. Shared Leadership promotes individual responsibility and collective accountability.

Accountability, the complete acceptance by individuals of the consequences of their actions, must exist at all levels if an organization is to reach its objectives. Decision making at the point of service runs counter to the traditional cultural norm in organizations, which has been to move accountability upward. It fundamentally shifts the way business is done. Traditional managers are anxious to maintain control over decisions as a way to minimize mistakes and this leads to a work force unwilling to make decisions without directives. For the individual, should a problem arise, someone else is to blame. Even the most enlightened managers can be infected by this insidious blaming approach.

"Blamability" blocks the Accountability Effect™. Once blamed, an individual's self-worth is damaged, and when blamed often enough or made the scapegoat, the harm to the individual can be irreparable. Moreover, the harm this causes to the organization is devastating. Not only does the blamed individual drop out but onlookers become risk averse and everyone fears to act, leading to failure to capitalize on new ideas or market opportunities.

Empowering all individuals with responsibility and accountability builds self-reliance as well as self-esteem. The results are a proactive, involved, committed and effective work force. Individuals take ownership of the organization's activities and trust replaces the traditional bureaucratic mire of policies and procedures.

Shifting or changing a culture to activate the Accountability Effect™ requires:

• Measuring how decisions are actually made and who takes responsibility for them.

• Assessing skill levels to determine both the willingness and ability of individuals to make decisions.

• Evaluating employee attitudes toward accepting accountability for decisions made.

• Making certain that decisions made are interconnected.

• Instituting feedback mechanisms to measure the quality of decisions made.

• Helping managers let go so that the Accountability Effect™ takes place.

Once the organization is committed to activating the Accountability Effect™, the whole system needs to be aligned so that all the organizational subsystems match individual and team accountabilities.

Value Hiring

For any organization to maximize its overall efficiency, it must be filled with people who match its values. Hiring a person without taking this into account and trying to force a fit does not work. It results in mutual disenchantment and a parting of the ways, and in the end, it is a costly way of doing business. At best, a mismatch ends in mediocre performance.

An existing organization that changes its culture will contain people who were comfortable with the old ways and cannot adapt to the new culture. These people will eventually leave but, if they do stay, they will covertly—and often unconsciously—sabotage Third Order Change. People who excelled in a structure that rewards individuals might pretend to be team players in a new team-driven culture, but if they do not value a team approach they will continue to resist. Others who are neutral may be influenced negatively. The stress that results is disruptive, taking energy away from successfully implementing the new culture.

People coming into an organization with knowledge of its new culture will, to some extent, self-select, but filling it with people who match requires Value Hiring. This requires creating clear job descriptions, carefully training interviewers and using evaluation tools that assess people's attitudes and behaviors as well as their technical skills.

Pay-For-Performance System

Organizational culture is made or broken by the strength of internal working relationships, and that strength depends on the quality of the individuals involved. A self-managed team environment, for example, cannot work if people are unwilling to share their expertise and work with others in a healthy give and take because of the way in which they are compensated. A Pay-for-Performance System aligned with the values of the organization, measuring both quantitative and qualitative components of performance, reinforces the desired culture. In a team approach, compensation criteria need to measure an individual's performance as a team player.

Interestingly, organizations have spent relatively little time aligning the formal reward subsystem to the relationship subsystem, relegating the latter to the realm of "soft stuff". This inattention has had a greater long-term impact on the bottom line than many of the cost cutting measures that have been the focus of organizations in recent years. Relationships, and indeed all of an organization's values, are reinforced by making them an economic issue. When individuals realize their compensation depends on both their financial objectives and their behaviors, they have a very different motivation. Moving one step further, to a holistic approach with a Pay-for-Performance System, causes collaboration to become more than rhetoric. When everyone gets a share of the pie, everyone's target becomes to enlarge the pie. Team-oriented organizations design Pay-for-Performance systems to compensate teams and not individuals.

In many traditional settings, the possibility of collaborative system-wide relationships among teams is slim. Units criticize each other, and often there is more internal than external competition. Finger pointing is the norm. "They" are at fault for missed deadlines, delays and lost sales. This blame-centered mentality poisons cooperation. Teams can do well only within their functional areas.

A team environment is fostered by encouraging systemic collaboration with the concept of extended teams—each area is a team, and each of these teams is a part of larger teams. They cannot be self-contained; all must interact positively. Tying in Pay-for-Performance when determining year end organizational results institutionalizes this concept.

Outcome Thinking®

In the past, organizations looked at problems and searched for the reason why they occurred and who was responsible. This problem-focus wasted precious time and money without moving the least bit closer to correcting the situation. In more recent years, studies have shown that high performing organizations have moved from a problem-focus to an outcome oriented approach in dealing with business issues. One of the most effective results-focused models is Outcome Thinking®. It raises six questions: what is the desired outcome; what criteria will be used to measure success; is it worth it; is it in one's control to achieve; what resources are needed; what action steps are necessary. The Outcome Thinking® Model compliments and reinforces the Accountability Effect™. Once action steps are defined, individuals take accountability for implementing them. They institute a timeline is instituted for each action step.

At IMC, everyone was trained to use the Outcome Thinking® Model. In addition to streamlining problem solving, a very significant added benefit was the language shifting that resulted. Everyone in the organization used phrases such as "what's your outcome?" and "what specific actions are you taking to achieve your outcome?" It was the use of the model that influenced the formation of action teams instead of committees since the former better matched the intent to be proactive and results-focused.

Communication Integrity

Historically, having information was equated with the amount of power and influence individuals had in an organization. What was communicated was selective, based on managerial decisions as to how much individuals needed to know. Information technology has changed this, making information readily available to everyone. In the future, organizations will be faced with an over-load of information. Communication Integrity is comprehensive, open, honest, relevant and fact-based. It means dismantling information privileges of the few. It introduces an organizational value that individuals can be trusted with the organization's "secrets," knowing as much or more than the competition knows. Individuals within the organization are the first to receive information. In some instances, they are asked for their ideas before any change takes place.

By itself, Communication Integrity can be the single most powerful fundamental change for building a value-driven organization. Concentrating on aligning the subsystems through this type of communication process enhances the organization's capabilities as well as fostering ongoing change.

Experiential Learning

Experiential Learning is a training technology of learning by doing. The model for Experiential Learning starts with an experience and proceeds to sharing reactions to the experience, followed by examining patterns and dynamics, generalizing and applying more effective work behavior.

According to a study done by *Success Magazine* in 1990, using Experiential Learning increases the potential for the learning to be internalized and used.[6] Learners are encouraged to be proactive, to take responsibility for their own learning. This high learner involvement capitalizes on the individuals' experiences and helps them more quickly assimilate new behaviors into their work environment.

A departure from the Socratic and lecture methods, Experiential Learning is more focused on the development of a common database for discussion. The activity becomes the basis for analysis. Most significantly, processing, generalizing and applying encourages the learners to internalize their learnings as well as practice new behaviors back on the job.

Well-planned Experiential Learning sessions can focus individuals toward specific, desired behaviors although, by its very nature, not all the learning outcomes may be as planned. Because the focus is on meanings internal to the learner, the actual applications will be based on the human interaction dynamics in the organization. For First Order Change, the Experiential Learning sessions are designed for technical skills development. For Second Order Change, the learning sessions are crafted on behavioral skill development.

Critical to learning sessions in Second Order Change are the follow-through mechanisms that reinforce and encourage new behaviors. As part of the training, individual and group behavioral contracting takes place. Individuals commit to action steps they are prepared to take immediately. These contracts are generally in writing so that, at a later point in time, the contracts can be reviewed to assess levels of behavioral effectiveness.

Conflict and Working Relationships

In the subsystem entitled Relationships, the organizational value shift is to do more than manage differences, it is to cause differences. Using conflict as an asset can increase an organization's capacity for innovation.

By definition, change means disruption. The idea of challenging the status quo, causing chaos—productive disruptions—is the essence of conflict. Coming to understand the mutual benefits of positive conflict helps an organization move from managing to anticipating to embracing change. The emphasis is on testing the unique contribution each individual can make against another individual's ideas. This testing of ideas, no matter how large or small, encourages risk taking, fosters a greater willingness to step forward and dramatically increases the organization's competitive capacity.

Relationships based on stimulating rather than suppressing work differences are better grounded in trust and openness. Hostilities among individuals disappear since everyone is operating from a base of mutual respect. An organization that values conflict is one that is highly charged, moving forward with a sense of urgency. Each new product or service is under intense scrutiny. Meeting the customers' needs is at the heart of the differences surfaced. Differences are work rather than personality driven.

Resolving conflicts becomes a matter of give and take. Once the majority of points is agreed, the issue is brought to a close and the end agreement or action accepted by everyone. Unless there is something new to be considered at some better date, the action(s) are implemented.

Peer Review and Upward Management Review

Sound working relationships depend to a large extent on open two-way communication. Allowing feedback on job performance at all levels of the organization recognizes the importance of day-to-day behaviors (Second Order Change). It helps improve the performance of all involved. This feedback comes between equals as Peer Reviews and from individuals to their managers as Upward Management Reviews.

Peer Reviews are one-on-one conversations between two people who work closely together. They capture the spirit of working relationships and the connectedness of individuals to the whole. Individuals discuss ways they interact, acknowledge strengths and seek to improve effectiveness. To foster ongoing feedback, the discussion is open and honest. Details are private and do not become part of a formal performance appraisal system. Instead, individuals are accountable to one another.

In *The Fifth Discipline*, Senge talks about the need for a learning environment.[7] Peer reviews are an effective method to institute a quality learning environment. They contribute to an atmosphere that demands uniformly excellent performance and behavior every day.

Upward Management Reviews give everyone in the organization an opportunity to provide feedback about the performance of managers. It gives managers information on how well they are supporting corporate values. Upward Management Reviews are most useful when everyone who is involved with particular managers—both those who report to them and those to whom they report—is given an opportunity to provide feedback. The end result is an expectation that managers will act on the feedback and make the systemic adjustments necessary.

Summary

• Organizations are systems requiring a holistic approach to bring about Second and Third Order Change.

• Each of the subsystems of an organization has an impact on the whole system, as each progresses through the three Orders of Change. Effective management and systemic planning enhances the ability of an organization to transform itself.

• The concepts used at IMC to manage its subsystems and effect Second and Third Order change included: Shared Leadership, the Accountability Effect™, Value Hiring, Pay-for-Performance, Outcome Thinking®, Communication Integrity, Experiential Learning, Conflict and Working Relationships and Peer and Upward Management Review.

PART II

Moving Below the Surface of the Iceberg:
A Case Study of the *Hospital of the Future* Project

> Ask every person if he's heard the story,
> And tell it strong and clear if he has not;
> That once there was a fleeting wisp of glory
> Called Camelot. . . .
>
> Don't let it be forgot,
> That once there was a spot,
> For one brief shining moment
> That was known as Camelot.
>
> — *Lerner and Loew*

Chapter 3. Health Care Delivery in the 1990s

Pressures for Change

Even as U.S. manufacturing companies became complacent after World War II, watched their market shares erode and clawed back to a competitive position, America's hospitals went along without competition or criticism. Commitments made to health care by government and labor unions starting in the 1940s, made health care a "right" and presented a blank check to the industry. It took 40 years before health care providers realized their account was badly overdrawn.

Before 1980, hospitals could basically charge whatever they wanted, secure in the knowledge that insurers would pay. But costs mushroomed, rising 166% during the decade, and, by the late 1980s, insurers—both the government and private companies—were looking for ways to cut costs. Soon the prices of procedures were being closely watched and doctors were being challenged to change the way they delivered care. Health Maintenance Organizations (HMOs) and Preferred Provider Organizations (PPOs) were becoming more prominent, the length of in-hospital treatment declined and the number of procedures handled on an outpatient basis increased.

By 1990, industry experts noted that many health care facilities were operating at a loss from inpatient services, staying afloat on outpatient services and ancillary income. The pressures cut into the hospital ranks. A parade of hospitals that were viable closed their doors.

Today, the U.S. health care system is knee-deep in crisis. Caregivers are struggling to stay ahead of changes that might take place when, and if, general agreement is reached on the best way to reform the system. At the beginning of President Bill Clinton's administration, the importance of health care delivery and the crisis of the system were trumpeted, but by the halfway point no political solutions were reached. The private sector, meanwhile, has been making its own solutions, trying to position itself for what may come. The health care industry is in a state of "permanent white water."[8]

In part controlling health care costs comes from reevaluating the elements of the health care system to determine what fundamental change is needed. How do hospitals maintain fiscal viability in the future. Reevaluation starts with realizing that there are only two categories of costs — people and supplies — and that people is by far the larger. In today's environment, the ground rules for running a successful hospital shift more quickly than for any other industry. Competition, long an unspoken word among hospitals, has become a very real force that must be part of each facility's planning for survival.

Thus the concerns, if not the responses, of hospital executives are being forced in line with those of executives in other industries. For any of these organizations to flourish amid such turmoil requires them to alter their fundamental outlooks—their structures must be able to respond readily to change. Yet, they resist mightily.

Ignoring signals from the marketplace, hospitals kept looking within their own ranks for guidance, listening to themselves instead of learning from other industries. This was aggravated by an attitude proclaiming their industry unique and declaring that no one from outside could understand them. On one level, the hospital business *is* different from other industries: it is more susceptible to criticism and self-examination than other industries since, by its very nature, it is required to care. Its executives must balance the Hippocratic Oath with bottom line profitability, technical progress and patient expectations.

In actuality, however, any number of the things hospitals do—some of them well, others not so well—are comparable to activities in other organizations, and hospitals can both learn and teach many lessons.

The concepts of the knowledge society and the knowledge worker underscore the hospital as an archetypal service-based organization; understanding hospitals was once suggested as a way of understanding the direction of society.[8] While hospitals may be a template for the service-based organization, they remain enveloped in traditions and structures that often interfere with their goals.

Thirty years ago, a typical hospital was led by a hospital administrator, a chief operating officer, a director of nursing, a chief financial officer, a public relations director and any number of department heads, supervisors and unit heads. Today, an administrator may be called an executive director, but the structure is, if anything, more calcified and layered, with vice presidents for patient services joining directors of nursing, vice presidents of finance supporting chief financial officers and directors of marketing in addition to those of public relations. Each department is an entity in and of itself. Lines are drawn, rivalries advanced and each claims to be the advocate of the patient.

Most doctors, meanwhile, are still not paid staff. They function as independent entities, though with the ultimate power of admitting or not admitting patients. Thirty years ago, for choosing a particular hospital, doctors were rewarded with such perks as free offices, specialized medical supplies and equipment, free food and loans. It was not unheard of for hospitals to buy a practice. These "bad boys of medicine" expected to be treated with deference. Today, though the doctors' leverage remains, there are fewer hospitals and their "bad boy" behaviors have been modified. In some places, laws have been passed cutting down on what hospitals can do to attract medical staff.

All in all, as modern technology has increased life expectancy, the ways in which care is delivered and patients are treated remain archaic. While a hospital's function is necessary, the industry has not learned how to respond to its changing environment. In this, hospitals are not alone.

The increasingly competitive world marketplace makes developing new organizations crucial. However, meeting this challenge requires time and commitment that starts at the top of the organization and permeates it at every level.

Toward Third Order Change

In looking toward the next century, the administratively obsolete and economically burdened health care industry is unlikely to leap the chasm of its culturally entrenched system to become progressive and financially successful entities without a "new order" of organizational values.

Efforts to model such an order began more than a decade ago with a series of projects developed in England and the United States in hospitals operated by American Medical International, Inc. (AMI), a for-profit hospital chain based originally in Los Angeles, California, and later in Dallas, Texas. These efforts culminated in the Irvine Medical Center, a facility that arose at the confluence of visionary leadership at AMI and the desire of the Orange County, California, community of Irvine to have its own hospital.

Summary

• The U.S. Health Care industry, long isolated from market forces by government and labor union commitments made after World War II, is faced with accelerating pressures to become more responsive to patient needs and economic reality.

• This historical isolation has created hospitals that are hierarchical and unresponsive.

• To meet current and future demands of a new competitive marketplace, hospitals must adopt a new set of organizational values that embrace and harness change.

Chapter 4. History of the Irvine Medical Center

Irvine, California, is an affluent and well-planned community on what was once a ranch owned by the Irvine family. Incorporated as a city in 1971, it has been carefully developed and is characterized by high population and employment growth and a relatively young, professionally-oriented population.

One goal of area residents was to develop Irvine's own community hospital, separate from the University of California at Irvine (UCI) and from other hospitals in the region. As 1990 closed, the quickly growing city of 110,000 had achieved that end, though the outcome differed in a number of ways from what was visualized when the building movement began.

The first movement for a community hospital came in the late 1960s from a group of Newport Beach physicians who wanted to build a facility in Newport Center. The community hospital would have been part of a biomedical complex. To support this project, several local leaders formed West World Medical Foundation in 1971. In 1973, the Irvine Company agreed to provide 18 acres for the hospital. Even though the Orange County Health Planning Council, then responsible for issuing hospital certificates of need, approved a 350-bed campus hospital, state restrictions, funding problems and shifting alliances kept it from being built.

Between 1973 and 1975, UCI won state approval to build a 200-bed campus hospital, but this became mired down in debate over building a new facility or buying the Orange County Hospital in Orange, some 20 minutes away under the best driving conditions. When funds to build were slashed by the state, the debate ended and the Orange County hospital became UCI Medical Center.

Meanwhile, West World continued efforts for a community hospital, and its differences with the university sharpened. By May 1977, West's proposal had been rejected by the planning council three times and the Irvine Company, under new ownership, withdrew the promised 18 acres. West World folded.

In late 1980, an active grassroots movement developed and 50 community members formed PICH (People for an Irvine Community Hospital) to back construction of a community-owned, community-controlled, not-for-profit hospital. In 1982, PICH, with nearby Hoag Memorial Hospital as a financial partner, created a not-for-profit corporation to build the Irvine Medical Center (IMC). Disagreement continued with the university, which blocked IMC's first building site on land owned by Irvine Valley College.

Both the university and IMC advanced plans for a new facility. In February 1983, IMC received the backing of the Irvine Company, which provided the 15 acres of land where the hospital has since been built. In July, the planning council recommended state approval of the IMC proposal and, in December, PICH received a certificate of need for a 177-bed hospital. Planning moved forward, with opening targeted for 1987.

Meanwhile, government cost containment efforts in health care led Hoag to reconsider the risks of operating a second hospital. Efforts to spread the risk by bringing Memorial Health Services of Long Beach into the partnership failed, and in April, Hoag withdrew from the project.

Anticipating the loss of Hoag, IMC had initiated talks with major nationwide health care providers and hospital chains. Several bid on the property and in June 1985, IMC granted the contract to American Medical International, Inc. (AMI). It took over in August.

Bringing in a for-profit health care chain changed the nature of the project, but the difficulty of raising the funds for a community-owned, nonprofit facility led IMC's backers to conclude that taking such a partner was the only way to get IMC built. PICH shifted its attention to grassroots health programs that, when the hospital opened, included subsidizing an active volunteer organization in its support.

Despite the emphasis on the community nature of the hospital, the university was an integral part of the project. UCI officials joined the IMC board in January 1985, and agreements providing for service arrangements between the two entities set the stage for a partnership that remained uneasy even after IMC opened. "Town versus gown" concerns continued to underlie the relationship and private practice concerns about university control periodically surfaced, often voiced by doctors who had not been around for the original controversy.

By July 1986, new plans were drawn for IMC. PICH and AMI decided that, in keeping with the community, the hospital would be strictly first class, in some senses as much a hotel as a hospital. All the rooms would be private, setting it apart to some extent from the large tertiary hospitals nearby. However, it would be the superior level of service and quality that was to distinguish IMC, drawing to it both patients and doctors.

Changes in AMI's leadership and structure, both locally and at corporate headquarters, caused progress to drag and changes in health care practice patterns toward shorter hospital stays led to corporate reevaluation of the project's viability. Despite statements in these analyses that the highly competitive area south of Los Angeles could not support another major hospital and that, if there were to be another hospital, a smaller facility would be more viable, the physical goals had been set and concern about damaging AMI's credibility kept the 177-bed facility on course.

By late 1986, these realities and the results of experiments in new care paradigms at other AMI hospitals caused the project leaders to reevaluate their organizational goals. Here, they found reason to change. Whereas they had planned a community hospital with a traditional structure, they decided to make this the flagship hospital of health care—the *Hospital of the Future*. It would be a revolutionary facility, both physically and operationally, taking into account state-of-the-art concepts in every aspect of its operation. Above all, it would be a source of ideas and inspiration, a proving ground for concepts to be extended to other AMI sites.

IMC planners decided to concentrate on specialties suited to its young, active community and set up service lines in orthopedics (catering to an active, sports-oriented lifestyle) and in women's and children's care (catering to young families).

On October 18, 1986, ground was broken with the opening targeted for October 1988. It was almost four years and many delays and changes later before IMC finally welcomed its first patients.

Then IMC quickly began to make its mark. Patients were thrilled with its service. Accolades and recognition it received indicated IMC had struck a chord. Hospital president John Gaffney was named "Administrator of the Decade" by the American Hospital Association.

The Joint Commission on Accreditation of Healthcare Organizations (JCAHO) was so impressed that it not only gave IMC full accreditation in late summer of 1990, it also identified IMC as having one of the best continuing quality enhancement processes in the country. Consistently during its first 18 months of operation, IMC had perfect scores on the AMI company-wide Patient Satisfaction Monitoring System, used to measure levels of patient and physician satisfaction.

Summary

• In the late 1960s, the idea of building a community hospital in Irvine, California, took root. Over the next 20 years, attempts to turn this dream into a reality met with a range of political and economic obstacles that threatened to destroy all hope of getting such a hospital built.

• In 1985, American Medical International, Inc. (AMI), a for-profit hospital chain, was authorized to build Irvine Medical Center (IMC)). AMI put in place a team that identified the need to create a new kind of facility in the saturated market and sought to gain competitive advantage by redefining health care delivery, using the latest philosophies and practices to create and maintain the *Hospital of the Future*.

Chapter 5. AMI's Prior Attempts at Changing a Hospital's Culture

The efforts that helped create a template for the *Hospital of the Future* grew from previous AMI projects in the United Kingdom and the United States. Each project provided valuable insights into what it takes to move from a traditional hierarchical way of operating to a more flexible, flat organization. Each highlighted aspects of the Three Orders of Change.

On both sides of the Atlantic Ocean, and transcending cultural and industry differences, the projects demonstrated that, if any organization is to make fundamental shifts and break with tradition, its leaders must:

- Understand the change process and the systemic nature of organizations.

- Recognize that, although hard to quantify in the short term, change and the organization's ability to manage it will benefit the organization's bottom line.

- Believe the vision can be realized.

- Recognize that an organization must invest in its individuals and build a value driven organization.

- Accept learning as a lifelong process and commit to creating a learning environment.

- Create high standards of performance with behaviors to reflect those standards.

The first project leading to the *Hospital of the Future* was with AMI's Eastern Division, where the concept of participative management was introduced in 1984. In today's management lexicon, participative management is described as the precursor to self-managed work teams. Each hospital in AMI's Eastern Division undertook a transformation of its management style by having its managers learn participative management skills. Their success was evidenced as the division's net revenues consistently led the company.

Building on this success, AMI took the concept to its United Kingdom operations, where it was embraced and expanded with the evolution of intact work teams and team networks. A training foundation of the management process, "Involvement Excellence Results (IER) Program," continues to influence the decision-making environment in the UK facilities.

In 1985 and 1986, at AMI's East Cooper Community Hospital in Mount Pleasant, South Carolina, and West Alabama General Hospital in Tuscaloosa, Alabama, a project began to transform the traditional, "business as usual" hospital mentality into a culturally progressive business attitude focusing on new behaviors needed to effect fundamental change.

East Cooper was a new institution and West Alabama an established facility. At both the aim was to shape a culture where change was created, accepted and managed to provide a competitive edge and an increased share of the marketplace. The idea was to measure whether a start-up facility was more receptive to change than a facility already operating. At West Alabama, the goal was to unobstruct the obstructed. At East Cooper, a culture was being defined from scratch, though with employees whose attitudes had been shaped at traditional facilities.

The starting place for developing the new cultures was stating intentions regarding mission, structure, policies, procedures, missions and goals and the subsequent training and development necessary to implement First Order Change. Making this First Order Change stick, however, required developing Second and Third Order Change mechanisms, to make the intentions into the fabric of the two organizations.

Both hospitals were approached as total systems and the same processes applied to each. Subsystems at both hospitals were examined in depth with analysis based on the premise that "nothing is sacred;" that by examining fundamental beliefs, the hospitals could determine their future.

Building a new culture started with aligning the daily beliefs of everyone on the executive team with the organization's guiding beliefs. A corporate steering committee from the two hospitals was established to measure progress. They concluded that to achieve First Order outcomes required strong, mature people characterized by Second Order qualities such as ability to take risks, flexibility and receptiveness to new possibilities, ability to manage change, individual self-confidence, and a perceived willingness to accept responsibility for their actions.

Each hospital started with high hopes, raising individual expectations. Each hospital demonstrated a tolerance—even eagerness for—change. Surveys and follow up interviews revealed the impact of culture building and of external forces helping to pinpoint approaches later used at IMC.

External forces brought the project to a grinding and dispiriting halt. The starting thesis that the hospital's Executive Director (ED) must be committed and be the lead change agent if there is to be meaningful and directed change was validated but the two EDs ran into an external leadership not committed to the change.

Unlike the UK operations, where leadership's commitment was consistent and pervasive, corporate dictates at East Cooper and West Alabama reversed the positive impact of the project and the EDs at both sites were replaced with people who had no vested interest in, or understanding of changing health care delivery. The new leaders effectively reverted back the facilities to traditional ways of operating, losing out on opportunities that arose from an ability to capitalize on change. In the UK operations, when EDs left, it was a corporate expectation that their successors continue a participative, open environment. This made the hospitals a valuable property that AMI sold profitably to a French company. Those hospitals continue to drive their organizational values. Their staffs are receptive and enthusiastic, excited by their environment and open to change.

Regardless of the outcome, East Cooper and West Alabama proved it is possible to develop a new hospital culture. They demonstrated it must become embedded over time if it is to survive. Perhaps most important, they proved that such a transformation could take hold both in a new hospital *and* in an established one.

Summary

• Prior to the decision to create the *Hospital of the Future* at Irvine, AMI had implemented aspects of new hospital cultures at several of its facilities in the U.S. and the United Kingdom. The increasingly ambitious efforts built on previous successes and involved changing both hospitals that were newly built and those having traditional management structures.

• The starting place with all of the hospitals was to put in place First Order Change while creating concepts to move them to Second and Third Order Change. Initial efforts in all facilities proved successful and those in the United Kingdom still flourish.

• The defining difference in implementing Second and Third Order Change was the degree of ongoing commitment of the hospital's leadership.

Chapter 6. First Order Change: Moving Toward the
Hospital of the Future

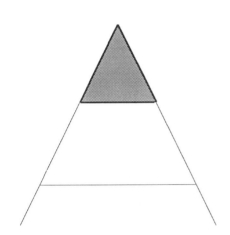

The learnings from East Cooper, West Alabama and the UK came together at IMC with the experiences of other progressive professionals. This group of self-described "visionary overachievers" set out to create a hospital that shattered the cultural mold traditional to the health care industry. IMC was to be a total reinvention, designed, both physically and culturally, without any preconceptions.

The goal of the team that built IMC was to deliver health care in a way that better met the demand of tomorrow's consumers. The team set out to create processes to improve health care delivery in single areas and to institute broader efforts to shift the culture of the entire institution. In looking at the *Hospital of the Future*, team members sought a creative, innovative environment. Doing this required reinventing the hospital by drawing a new covenant between manager and employee, based in new corporate values.

Team members worked with elements of the past projects and their experiences at other hospitals, integrating them to effect Second Order Change. They used Value Hiring methodology, Pay-For-Performance and Outcome Thinking®, and shared accountability processes. They drew on their understanding of the need for commitment and consistency and developed comprehensive communication to reinforce the desired culture. They added such concepts as service lines, language and a *Service Excellence*™ philosophy that defined high standards of performance. Many excellent hospitals had applied one or two of these concepts, but none had applied a systemic approach toward full-scale revolution.

Defining the Best: What Would It Be Like If It Were Perfect?

The essence of the *Hospital of the Future* project was to build a profitable, quality-driven health care facility. This required installing processes in which people felt empowered to achieve excellence, allowing them to be creative, to learn from their mistakes and to maintain their self-esteem in spite of a constantly changing external environment. This also involved challenging every belief, concept and value within the traditions, habits and experience of hospital personnel.

The health care professionals who designed IMC wanted to take the best of their experience in traditional settings and build a hospital that set the standards for the industry into the next century. The professional expertise of that core team included nursing, finance, physician services, marketing, organizational development and education and training.

This core team first met in the fall of 1986. The first question it asked itself, and the question it kept coming back to was "What would it be like if it were perfect?"

To answer this question and create IMC's future, members explored in depth their collective personal values and experiences with an eye on creating a nontraditional collective value system. This critical analysis was predicated on shifting paradigms—the premise that "nothing is sacred." Here was an opportunity to start with a clean slate and build the kind of hospital they had only dreamed of previously.

They established IMC's working framework:

- **As a vision:**   *Service Excellence*™ through teamwork

- **As a mission:**   Decision making at the point of service

- **As a methodology:**   Shared Leadership

- **As a motto:**   Spirit of Service

They declared IMC's shared organizational values:

• Shared knowledge empowers us to make decisions.

• We recognize and appreciate that our differences are our strengths and that each team member makes valuable contributions.

• Participation, enthusiasm and pride in ourselves enhance our decisions.

• Service to each other is our way of doing business.

• Teamwork and collaboration throughout our medical center are essential to achieving our vision.

• Successful outcomes are reached when organizational and personal values and beliefs are aligned.

• Trust in ourselves and in each other encourages us to take risks and to grow.

• We make decisions that are consistent with both our financial objectives and with federal and state regulations.

• As team members, we are individually accountable and responsible for the care of our patients and their families.

They wrote a mission statement and defined how each of the statement's five elements applied to IMC stakeholders: the board of directors, physicians, patients, team members, volunteers, community, AMI, its parent corporation, UCI and the shareholders. The mission statement was added to everyone's business cards and used as another reminder that IMC was committed to "walk the talk."

They then organized IMC's functions to take First Order Change and move toward Third Order Change. The core team wanted a hospital that was known for *Service Excellence*™, with an environment that was friendly to patient, doctor and staff. To live IMC's "Spirit of Service" motto, they needed a working environment that allowed for job satisfaction and pride.

They took the concept of Shared Governance, long used in nursing, and expanded it to Patient Case Management as a way of life for everyone involved in the hospital's operations. Rather than traditional "employees," they sought out proactive, involved and committed "team members" whose ownership of the shared corporate values made the new culture successful. To achieve this, they implemented a unique Value Hiring process and committed themselves to a comprehensive training and development program to give every member necessary team skills, and to cross-train individuals where appropriate. The process was to be forever, ongoing and constantly renewed and reemphasized.

Developing IMC's culture started with the core team. As others were hired, there was a limited window of opportunity to align the corporate values with individual values. The desire was to cause this alignment before the hospital opened. A heavy emphasis was placed on training and development.

Workshops were designed to influence the organizational values. These workshops also were team building sessions, encouraging connectiveness and collaboration.

Team members took behavioral inventories and then shared the information, which gave them an appreciation of the different ways they saw situations and how to work with differences to make them strengths rather than divisive weaknesses. They learned skills needed to be leaders of a cutting-edge organization. As new members joined, they were integrated into this team environment.

The workshops laid the foundation for developing the hospital. As IMC came closer to reality and the nuts-and-bolts demands of its start-up took greater chunks of time, the organization cut back on the frequency of the workshops. While a schedule of regular get-togethers, even less frequently, was valuable, the basic bonds between the team members were well forged and relationships and interactions were sound.

IMC's product was its service. To turn this into a competitive advantage required *Service Excellence*™, which they defined as giving people more than they expected, starting with quality medical care delivered by first-rate professionals. To do this, the hospital's organization needed to be proactive, responsive and resourceful. Decisions would be made at the point of service, with involvement of patients and their families.

The pressure for this kind of firsthand authority presents hospitals with a challenge. To move decision making to the point of service means flattening the organization's hierarchical structure, reconfiguring hospital functions and, most importantly, enforcing accountability as a value.

The core team recognized that the most important person in the system is the one who comes in contact with the customer, and that everyone directly or indirectly impacts the quality of care.

Inventing the Hospital's Structure

To structure IMC, the core team raised critical questions. It took the typical hospital and reexamined every single function, asking, What value does this function add? Is there a better way to do it? The results were to eliminate the entire middle management level of the hospital; to combine functions; to add new, more relevant functions, and to flatten the structure for the total organization to six layers: president, vice presidents, team directors, patient case managers, specialists and associates.

Flatter organizations are more empowering. The fewer people looking over someone's shoulder, the more likely it is that decisions will be made quickly and effectively at the point of service. This naturally gives individuals more opportunity to act independently. At IMC, the flatter organization with its shorter reporting lines emphasized a commitment to service by placing closer to the top persons who interact directly and frequently with the patients. Housekeeping and dietary people, who clean the rooms and prepare and serve the food, are usually relegated to the background in traditional settings even though they often have more impact on the quality of a patient's stay than doctors. Patients may see someone from housekeeping as often as they see a nurse, yet the importance of these interactions to patients and their comfort has been downplayed or forgotten entirely.

In addition to flatness, the criteria for IMC's structure were that it:

• Reflect IMC values;

• Be profitable and cost effective ;

• Be defined but flexible and innovative, be integrated and non-bureaucratic;

• Allow decision making at the lowest level;

• Be patient driven and physician friendly;

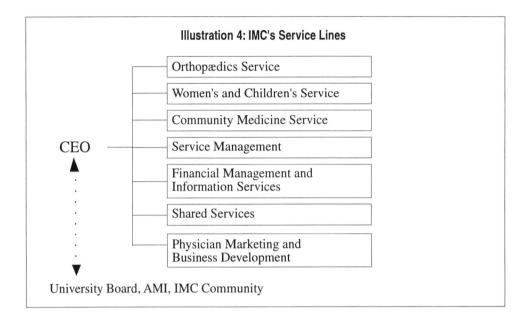

Illustration 4: IMC's Service Lines

CEO

- Orthopædics Service
- Women's and Children's Service
- Community Medicine Service
- Service Management
- Financial Management and Information Services
- Shared Services
- Physician Marketing and Business Development

University Board, AMI, IMC Community

• Contain only positions that each have add-on value;

• Provide career growth opportunities; and

• Be simple and understandable.

Operationally, Irvine was divided into seven interdependent service lines (Illustration 4), each headed by a vice president who reported directly to the president and each designated as a profit center.

In its marketing analysis, IMC identified three major medical service areas—orthopædics, women's and children's, and community medicine—and each was served by a separate service line. These areas were chosen based on the expected needs of the Irvine community.

The service lines interacted as separate mini-businesses with financial targets tied to overall profitability of the hospital. To ensure collaboration among the service lines rather than competition, meeting financial targets as individual lines did not result in profit sharing unless the whole hospital was successful. This made each vice president accountable for helping the others in such common areas as financial management, service management and physician services.

The other four service lines encompassed the support and indirect functions needed by the direct care areas. Their role was to be efficient, low-cost vendors to the medical lines. The nurses and physicians, plus such groups outside the hospital as insurers, were considered customers and the foremost job of these lines was to meet their requirements. Creating an internal vendor/customer relationship was intended to eliminate turf battles with technicians in the ancillary areas by clearly defining relationships.

Service Management was not limited to serving patients. It was the embodiment of all those areas that affect a customer, internal or external: patient, physician or team member. It embraced environmental services, health services, and hotel services including the hospital cafeteria. It included internal services, such as human resources, quality assurance, education and volunteers. A number of these areas have traditionally been relegated to the bottom of hospital organizational charts and here the flattening of the structure provided them with more immediate access to the top of the structure—a loud, clear message about their importance at IMC.

Segments within each line were grouped under team directors, reporting to the vice president. Directors were each responsible for a group of services and were instructed to act as coaches for their group of related services. For example, under Service Management, patient support services (registration, social services, discharge planning, patient transportation, the chaplain and parking) were one team. The team director for hotel services also oversaw engineering and food nutrition. In Community Medicine, one team director was responsible for the medical and surgical areas and another for critical care. Other areas, such as quality assurance, patient satisfaction and risk management, stood alone and reported directly to their service line's vice president.

The team directors' role in the Shared Leadership structure was basically as coaches of teams in hospital units. Because of the lack of hierarchy, some observers voiced concern that the Joint Commission on Accreditation of Healthcare Organizations (JCAHO) might require alterations in the nursing administration line of command before it granted accreditation. These concerns proved groundless; the accrediting body commended the quality of IMC's patient care.

There is no single way to structure an organization but once a structure is decided, and provided all the subsystems are aligned with the structure, it must be allowed to stay in place until individuals become committed to it. This gives the minor adjustments and internal interactions a chance to settle out and allows the structure's impact to be fully evaluated.

Within IMC's structure, strategic planning methods acknowledged change through Shared Leadership. The planning process started with five Shared Leadership Strategic Action Teams (SLSATs), each concentrating on a strategic priority: (1) strategic development, (2) culture and team member development, (3) medical staff development, (4) cost/efficiency management, and (5) net revenue growth. Each team was responsible for a short-term (12-month) and a long-term (three-year) plan. Both were to be updated annually, with the second year of the previous long-term plan, appropriately modified, becoming the next short-term plan.

The plans set forth priorities and the criteria for implementing and measuring them. They laid out financial strategies, including return on investment (ROI), implementation strategies and capital funding requirements.

Each SLSAT consisted of representatives of four of the seven service lines. This placed representatives of each service line on three teams. Members of the board of directors and of the medical staff were assigned to each. A vice president acted as facilitator for each team and participation of team members was encouraged.

The plans were brought to the executive management team for joint approval, with discussion focusing on the big picture but supported, as needed, by details the SLSATs provided on request. Each plan was evaluated according to an agreed upon standardized criterion and, once consensus was achieved, each was to be shared throughout the hospital and implemented. The SLSAT's would continue to track the plans, putting together quarterly updates on their progress and remaining accountable for the results.

It was clear that to succeed, as with all other facets of a major change, this whole strategic planning process had to be driven from the top and required the commitment of the CEO.

Implementing Shared Leadership

Shared Leadership as a participatory process requires information in the same way that democracy requires an informed electorate. Team members cannot withdraw solely into job-specific data. They cannot ignore outside forces that shape the organization.

IMC's plan to implement Shared Leadership recognized it as an ongoing cycle of interconnected events and activities. It was implemented in four phases of learning, each lasting for one year, with the intent that, after four years, the corporate values were to be fully integrated throughout the hospital. At that time, team members were to handle all of their area's administrative functions which conventionally are handled by managers or supervisors.

At all phases and levels, there was an evaluation system to determine the progress of Shared Leadership. Criteria for success were specifically adhered to and defined. The moving, ever-changing criteria used by many organizations only serve to undermine their ability to manage change, much less to introduce a fundamental change such as Shared Leadership.

Development Phases

Phase I included hiring, acculturation, specific performance expectations and a training and development curriculum that gave each team member the skills to implement Shared Leadership. Individuals were introduced to the process of self-scheduling. Actual self-scheduling began as teams were ready to accept responsibility. After the initial training modules were completed, responsibility for reinforcing and enhancing individual proficiency went to the service lines.

Phase II included a fully implemented quality assurance program, a central supplies ordering system, a complete set of policy and procedure manuals and defining financial targets for each self-managing team. Every team member was trained to understand IMC's financial requirements and the budget process. Each team and service area participated in selection and purchase of supplies and equipment.

Phase III included peer reviews, upward management reviews, continuing quality improvement processes and team recommendations setting standards for hiring new personnel. In addition, interdepartmental disciplinary boards were established. Individuals were to be participating in peer reviews and contributing to the hospital business plan.

Phase IV included finalizing the processes throughout the hospital and evaluating how well Shared Leadership was integrated. Emphasis was on interdisciplinary staffing, cross-training and creating team incentives and research and development projects. Individual team members were to develop new skills, growing professionally and personally.

Shared Leadership in Action

On a daily basis, nurses cannot deal only with patient care or with administration. Shared Leadership requires that they be involved in the actual running of their service, that they help with supplies, staffing and quality assurance. The detail work reserved for traditional department managers devolves in part to administrative associates, and in part to each nurse on a rotating basis. At the same time, it requires all to be caregivers and current on nursing practices. Overall, this means that every nurse will be involved in patient care the majority of the time and every nurse will be involved in administration some of the time.

Prompt Quality Service at the Bedside

IMC's ideal of delivering quality care was embodied in its approach to patient case management. This manifestation of decision making at the point of service and the empowerment that arose from it clearly demonstrated the Accountability Effect™.

Medical care serves a hospital's primary clients, patients and their families. The hospital is there for them, not for the convenience of management and administrators. There must be consistency in delivering quality care and in the ability to make decisions about that care quickly and with a minimum of service-delaying red tape. Efficiency is important, not only for effective care but because of the need for it forced on hospitals by the changing face of health care. With the average length of a hospital stay shrinking, patient care providers need an environment in which they can make decisions for their patients on the spot. They cannot wait for the head nurse or a supervisor to be available or for a decision to go up to a Director of Nursing because it is a variation on a policy or procedure.

The registered nurses on IMC's core team asserted that even the most up-to-date nursing systems they had worked with lacked the key elements of consistency and direct patient care decision making. Accordingly, they developed a system for delivering comprehensive care that increased efficiency and built in accountability for every caregiver. "Case managers"—registered nurses assigned to the patients and working with their physicians—made 99 percent of the decisions, leaving only a few to be handled by the service line vice presidents or the hospital's president. They coordinated multidisciplinary care delivery teams that included everyone needed to provide comprehensive and consistent care for each patient. Membership of each specific team depended on an individual patient's needs.

The patient case management system, which benefited patients by fostering decision making by the people working most closely with them, increased the autonomy of the caregiver and the satisfaction of patients and their families. It communicated to all team members a consistent plan providing quality, individualized care with all expenses tracked. Perhaps most important, it was proactive, providing a ready source of treatment information to patients and members of their families, keeping them constantly involved.

The concept of an RN patient case manager with a split role of clinical practice and administrative responsibility was a unique element of the IMC structure. The case manager had the current clinical expertise to deliver direct patient care, plus the authority to make administrative decisions for groups of patients without having to go through layers of supervisors, head nurses and nursing directors who may have been in predominantly administrative roles so long that their clinical skills had dulled.

At IMC, case managers and nurse specialists spent 80 percent of their time tending to patients with the rest devoted to administration. Through Shared Leadership, other team members took charge of administrative tasks such as ordering supplies, stocking and checking inventory and meeting regulatory requirements. Educational programs bolstered the self-management skills of the teams. The case managers made decisions on every aspect of a patient's care. They acted on the seemingly trivial but still annoying issues that make a difference in patients' attitudes, so they had the authority to advocate for patients and their families. Using *Outcome Thinking®*, they defined what they needed and facilitated acquisition of resources and services.

In exchange for this responsibility, each case manager was given great autonomy, the kind of rewarding role expected in the long-term growth pattern of specialists in services-based organizations. Nurses have complained for years that they want more collaboration with physicians, that they want consistency, that they don't want their assignments made just because of where the patient's room is located. IMC's structure looked at the expertise of each nurse, with case managers specializing in disciplines such as neurology, oncology or telemetry.

For physicians, there was the advantage of going to a single person for information about their patients. Some initial confusion at being unable to find a case manager was rapidly offset for most physicians by having one person they could call 24 hours a day. In addition, nurses on the care team were fully briefed on each case, using two carefully developed tools — the Multidisciplinary Treatment Plan and the Patient Pathway — that modeled the care needed for each patient, communicated patient status and highlighted what needed to be followed up with the physician.

How the Case Management System Worked

The case manager's accountability started from the time a patient was admitted. The first step was a complete patient assessment. If the case manager was not available, the primary nurse specialist assigned to the team did the assessment. Based on the information developed, the team prepared a specific plan for each patient—a detailed guideline for the patient's course of treatment. While every hospital has nursing plans, IMC's precisely mapped the treatment steps for each day of a patient's stay for 75 percent of all diagnoses.

This gave patients — and their families — information that allowed them to participate intelligently in their own care. It also cut down on late nightcalls from the hospital to physicians.

After the plan was confirmed by the caregiving team and the patient, the case manager matched it with an appropriate Patient Pathway, a synopsis of the total care plan, based on the agreed treatment plan for a particular ailment and used as a road map for the course of the hospitalization. With most of the treatment plans and pathways standardized, the process was easily put on computer, creating a day-to-day, shift-by-shift working communication tool to track the interventions done for the patient. The case manager updated the plan based on physician orders, patient acuity and team members' input, so the specifics of the plan remained fluid throughout the course of a hospitalization. The two tools generated the patient schedule for each day, tracking patient progress and ensuring that everyone involved remained readily able to determine the patient's status.

IMC's patient case management system, which also was used for outpatient care plans, was designed to manage effectively the length of a hospital stay, to maximize patient and family awareness and involvement in treatment, to increase the autonomy of the treatment team and to improve control of hospital resources. By coordinating all functions and defining standards of practice, it also aimed to decrease malpractice issues. X-rays and other tests were ordered for the needs of the patient, not for the protection or convenience of the physicians and facility. This made the hospital more marketable to insurers and debt payers.

At all times, the case manager maintained a broad view of the way in which care was delivered and was professionally accountable for both cost and quality of its delivery. The system was supported by team members throughout the hospital. The direct members of the team—the patient care providers—monitored trends and changes in care and maintained team standards and commitment to quality management. Team members in nonclinical areas supported and marketed the system, sold the model to physicians, maintained team standards by selecting new team members and retaining existing one and communicated patient needs and progress toward outcomes.

As to physicians, the younger ones tended to be more enthusiastic about the concept than the older ones. Some of the older physicians worried that care plans could force them into a "cookbook" style of medicine or that too much documentation would actually foster malpractice suits. However, as doctors actually worked with the patient case management system, most found it beneficial to patients as well as themselves.

Summary

• The core team of progressive professionals which developed the *Hospital of the Future* drew on its best practice experiences, the proven innovation of previous AMI projects and the healthy belief that no tradition is sacred. Their goal was to set the standards of care and service for the health care industry into the next century.

• A flattened organizational structure is more empowering, and IMC's structure emphasized its commitment to service by placing decision making at the point of service. The structure encouraged cooperation among all teams by making their results interdependent.

• Shared Leadership was implemented using a series of phased training targets designed to instill new cultural practices over a four-year period. This program opened communication pathways, established team thinking and developed individual accountability.

• IMC's case management system established care giving teams for each patient, providing central responsibility, a predictable yet individualized plan of care and maximum participation and reassurance for patients and their families.

Chapter 7. Second Order Change

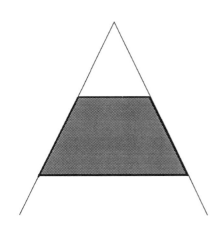

Changing the culture of an existing organization deals with the reactions of people who are used to a certain way doing things. The challenge for the organization in Second Order Change is to guide these people through the psychological aspects of change.

Starting a new organization that differs from the organizational norms of its industry is an even greater challenge since it carries similar psychological upheaval — without the professional anchor — plus the stresses inherent in any new organization. Bringing together several hundred strangers to do jobs at which they are skilled and experienced but in a new environment is unsettling. Whether in an existing facility or a new one, fundamental change depends on peoples behavior.

Finding and Orienting the Right People

Major innovations require people with a range of talents. Visionaries dominate an organization in its planning stage but become a smaller proportion of the team when the plan becomes operational.

Concepts of empowerment, such as Shared Leadership, emphasize different qualities than do traditional settings and implementing them can be easier if the right people are participating. Yet, when a vision differs from the industry's norm, the likelihood of discomfort grows, no matter how careful the hiring process. People finding this uncharted ground unnavigable will leave without prejudice when they find themselves lost. Even when turnover is expected, however, it is a setback to achieving organizational objectives.

At IMC, turnover during the first months of operation was upwards of 30 percent. This magnitude was anticipated, though no one was sure exactly how much would take place. There was little information on new hospitals since relatively few were being built.

Many of the people who entered the system sought to see if the *Hospital of the Future* was where they wanted to work. Those who saw it was not, left and each time team members left, costs increased and assimilation of processes and procedures was set back.

Predictably, the people who planned IMC did not all remain to implement their plans. For some, the fun—and their greatest effectiveness—was in planning, not in maintenance. It was critical for their replacements to accept IMC's values and culture and be integrated into the leadership promptly so the consistency with which those values reached team members was unimpaired.

Finding team members in the long term was expected to become less difficult, since the kind of people seeking out an established IMC were likely to be more skilled and have a lot more initiative than the industry had traditionally sought and used. They were likely to be looking for the kinds of challenges offered by the *Hospital of the Future*, to warrant the label "visionary overachiever" coined by IMC's core team.

The Search

Assembling the right staff to help leaders through change required a well-thought-out selection process followed by intense acculturation training. Picking people whose beliefs were in line with the beliefs of the organizers was intended to make achieving Second Order Change easier.

To enhance the selection process, IMC provided clear, precise job profiles and used behavioral assessment tools that provided insights into how individuals were apt to deal with change and participation. The profiles and tools indicated the receptiveness of participants—both those on board and potential new hires—to new ideas, a receptiveness that was reasonably likely since many of the persons interviewing were attracted, at least in part, by the prospect of working in a revolutionary environment. The information gathered in the interview process further improved the likelihood that individuals who were brought in had not only the technical skills required but also a propensity for embracing change as an opportunity.

IMC sought to build a start-up team of 450 people with substantial experience. While experience was expected to be desirable at all times, it was especially important when the hospital was preparing to open. Start-up team members generally had a minimum of five years in health care; some had been supervisors in other hospitals. IMC's first task was having everyone to "dance together," melding people with a range of generally traditional experiences into an effective, cohesive operation.

One way IMC found new people was through team members already on board. Openings were routinely posted and published at the hospital and team members were encouraged to refer people they knew.

With the right people aboard, the challenge was to orient them to the new culture and make them part of the structure that would sustain it. To do this, IMC instituted an extensive acculturation process with ongoing reinforcements. Key to this was creating a new appropriate language.

Language

Language—descriptors that balance what is desirable with what is acceptable to the community—is the great enforcer of intent. It is critical in establishing a new culture since it helps define perception of the organization. Language reinforces behaviors. In an organization, it aids Third Order Change, but language cannot be fully effective unless backed by substantive behavioral changes.

Implementing a new vocabulary is most effective when done all at once, despite the probability of initial confusion. To be effective, it requires substantial publicity, especially for people such as patients and physicians who are less constantly in contact with the system. Over time, the vocabulary becomes second nature to everyone involved.

Accordingly, IMC developed a vocabulary unique among hospitals to emphasize its values of service and collaboration. To emphasize its commitment to service, IMC developed health care segments called *service lines*. This was further emphasized in the nonclinical lines, Service Management, Shared

Services, Financial Management and Information Services, Physician Services and Business Development and by the titles of ancillary areas where *medical information services*, *surgical services*, *food and nutrition services* and *emergency services* replaced the traditional *medical records*, *operating room*, *dietary department* and *emergency room*, respectively.

The collaborative nature of the work environment was embodied in teamwork. To emphasize Shared Leadership, collaboration and interdependence as the hallmark of the way care was delivered, IMC replaced the words *employee* and *staff* with *team member*. Use of *boss* and *subordinate* was forbidden.

Organizationally, a perfect IMC would have no titles. However, necessity dictated that the structure have some form, and the core team concluded that the hospital administrator be called *president* because this title equated with the comparable leadership role in the business community. Medical staff designations also remained traditional, since physicians are outside a hospital's formal structure.

The rest of the designations followed the flatness of the organization chart, but were not just a surface change. They reflected the difference in people's roles. The most dramatic title shift was made for nursing. In traditional settings, nursing has a hierarchical structure headed by a director of nursing through department heads, unit heads and charge nurses. Decisions are for the most part hierarchically driven. Having *case managers* instead of head nurses defined a position with very different duties and responsibilities.

Designation as *specialists* and *associates* further created a cooperative equality, emphasizing that within Shared Leadership, all nurses (and everyone else, for that matter) made decisions within their areas of expertise without having to turn to a supervisor. All team members—whether president or nutrition associate—worked at a point of service and were held accountable for their decisions. Each was there to provide service and support to customers.

In the case of the president or a vice president, the "customers" were their direct reports. The president also acted as liaison with the hospital's board and all the external licensing agencies and the corporate parent. These interfaces were the relevant points of service.

Other language changes that supported the new culture included:

• *Action teams* rather than *committees*. This was intended to emphasize the proactive nature of the culture.

• *Financial specialist* rather than *controller*. This carried the expectation that the financial specialist would proactively monitor fiscal trends as well as expenditures.

• *Administrative associates* rather than *secretaries*. Their role was to help maintain linkages throughout the hospital.

• *Nutrition associates*. Their role was not only to deliver food to patients but to educate the patients regarding nutrition.

• *Environmental service associates* rather than *housekeepers*. Their role was to assess the overall environment of the hospital and bring forward ideas that were both ecologically sound and enhanced *Service Excellence*™.

• *Patient care plan* rather than *nursing care plan,* emphasizing the customer rather than the provider.

• *Imaging* rather than *X-ray,* describing a more diverse state-of-the-art technology.

• *Lounge* rather than *waiting room.*

• *Call system* rather than *nurse call system.*

Value messages were also given nonverbally. For example, there was a cafe, open to both visitors and team members. Eliminating the traditional, artificial barrier of separate cafeterias emphasized teamwork and the importance of provider/customer interaction.

Most important in nonverbal communications was the way the senior people modeled and demonstrated their commitment to the culture. IMC's president was available, without hierarchical barriers of closed doors. He was very comfortable walking the halls and chatting with everyone, complimenting people, promoting team spirit and gently exhorting them to do their best. During orientation for new team members, he told them that mistakes were okay. him. He explained that it was grounds for dismissal if they used either of two phrases: "That's not my job" and "We've always done it this way."

He modeled the "everything's my job" philosophy. One lunchtime, for example, a delay had led to a long line in the cafeteria, so he went behind the counter and served sandwiches to the people who wanted them. "It only takes 30 seconds," he said. Throughout the hospital, signs reading "I do windows" were a reminder that everyone working at IMC was accountable for all hospital operations.

The Cultural Buy -In

How well newcomers buy into a culture depends to a large extent on how the first messages they are given emphasize the culture's beliefs. At IMC, the acculturation program was named TEAM TIES, an acronym with each letter representing a corporate value:

Teamwork

Excellence

Attitude

Mission

Trust

Initiative

Education

Service

The name itself was a product of the culture, with team members contributing their thoughts to naming it something other than just "the orientation program." The program emphasized attitudes and skills that a Shared Leadership system requires.

The 14- hour program was spread over four days and complemented the Buddy System, a process that paired new team members with "veterans" who welcomed them and guided them through the precepts of the organization. The Buddy System was designed to establish an ongoing mentoring relationship that was to last as long as both parties were at the medical center. The veterans painted the cultural picture of IMC for their rookie partners. They wrote a "Rookies" article for the newsletter, ensuring that each new team member was introduced to the entire hospital team. In the process, they learned to know their buddies better.

While some people did not take readily to long-term mentoring, others easily formed the special "buddy bonds" of a lasting relationship. All found that the system helped ease their entry into the *Hospital of the Future*.

In the days immediately before IMC opened, when 450 rookies were hired in 45 days, the Buddy System was badly strained, as were all of the interviewing and orientation mechanisms. For the Buddy System, this meant newcomers were shortchanged. Instead of buddying being one-on-one, it became five rookies or more to one veteran, which meant extra effort for the veterans until things settled down. When the number of "old-timers" was again greater than the number of rookies, a one-on-one program was resumed.

In an effort to at least partially offset this pre-opening pressure, other activities were sponsored to complement formal, ongoing acculturation. Some continued to be useful in "normal" times. These were designed to acquaint everyone and make a start on developing the relationships and trust levels that evolve in an older facility during weeks and months of working together. They included social gatherings, team events and meetings for single areas of the hospital and for the hospital as a whole.

For physicians, initial acculturation activities centered on medical staff action teams. When IMC opened, there were 35 such groups, which is high for any hospital. A 24-hour hotline was established to answer physicians' questions and respond to their needs. All this activity was part of the recruitment process to generate excitement and physician involvement.

Another key facet of the acculturation program was to change beliefs regarding conflict. This offshoot to empowerment introduced conflict as an asset. The corporate value was to respect differences. People were taught how to capitalize on these differences to create greater synergy as well as learning new ways to resolve disputes.

As much as possible, team leaders encouraged direct resolution of conflicts between parties. They basically turned complainers back out the door to handle problems directly. This process was not easy. For many people, the natural approach to conflict is to be mad behind the back of someone who offends them, discussing their anger with everybody else. This, of course, just allows resentment to grow. Insisting that people go to the person they are having trouble with keeps communication lines open and leads to mutual trust.

Action Teams

Acculturation, of course, is only a starting point. If culture is to be meaningful and not merely a veneer, there must be constant feedback and activities to reinforce it. In addition to language, this comes from mechanisms that embody the desired culture.

Central to this process, and crucial to any empowered organization, is communication. This must be constant and in all directions, flowing freely across disciplines without getting bogged down in hierarchical posturing. To reinforce its culture, IMC instituted action teams and a variety of programs designed to make behaviors pervasive and reactions second nature. The teams included issue action teams and a Vision Action Team (VAT), charged with protecting IMC's culture.

Issue action teams were charged with tasks that affected more than one nursing unit. They dealt with such topics as budget, quality management, ethics, education, health care delivery and inservice relationships. Each was composed of volunteers from each patient care unit, who sat on teams for six-month terms.

VAT had a rotating membership with staggered terms of less than a year. Its structure and size evolved, starting with five people from different areas of IMC's operations and adding people from the medical center as well as representatives of the medical staff, PICH, the board of directors and hospital volunteers.

VAT developed a range of programs devoted to continuing cultural education. One of the first was the Food for Thought Hour, an ongoing lunchtime program held the first Thursday of each month, each time facilitated by a different volunteer. The program was established to "help motivate members to high levels of service, creativity and fiscal accountability." The lunches were brown-bag, one-hour educational or motivational presentations that promoted IMC culture, service and skill development or were medical or health related.

They included films, videotapes and speakers from IMC and outside, and each ended with group discussion.

Similar lunch meetings were held periodically in every department. They discussed policy trends, current hospital events and ongoing education. As with the VAT-sponsored lunches, responsibility for leading rotated among team members.

Another feature of lunch sessions was "barometer" checks of the culture's status. These resulted in a range of changes in hospital operations. Attendees were typically asked to rank the three best and worst things about working for IMC. They were also asked to list the most important things they would change. Their suggestions resulted, among other things, in the use of cloth diapers rather than disposables and in the composition of prepackaged sterilized trays, both of which saved the hospital monies and were environmentally friendly.

VAT developed a suggestion program called the Brain Bowl. Suggestion programs can do wonders for involvement, but only if tied into an efficient feedback system. The most important element is promptly acknowledging receipt of the idea to the person submitting it. Later, the person must be told the decision that was made, either to use the idea or not, and the reasons for not using an idea must be explained. If the reasons address broader considerations of organizational connectiveness, they can help the person become more sensitive to a total systems approach to doing business. For example, telling someone an idea is good but that it is necessary to set priorities for using funds can dispel the ideas that organization leaders don't have anyone to answer to or make decisions arbitrarily.

At IMC, VAT removed suggestions from the Brain Bowl weekly and acknowledged them within 24 hours. Where possible, a decision was made within a week and if this was not possible, a report on its status was made weekly. Ideas and actions taken were reported in the biweekly IMC newsletter, *StethoScoop,* and Brain Bowl awards were given. Suggestions, where appropriate, were pushed quickly to reality. VAT also contacted people who offered suggestions that were not used and explained why.

VAT was also responsible for IMC's version of Upward Management Reviews, conducting random face-to-face interviews regarding leaders' performance. Other VAT programs included:

- A staff survey to glean ideas for processes and programs to enhance organizational performance

- A reference library of resources available at IMC.

- Half-day follow-up sessions to training programs to confirm application of skills.

- Brainstorming sessions.

VAT encouraged feedback on IMC's culture. Periodically, it asked team members for their opinions on different culture-related statements as a way of monitoring how the culture was doing and determining where the VAT needed to focus its attention.

Culture Checks

In addition to these teams, IMC was constantly checking on the state of the hospital, monitoring and checking attitudes and actions. The idea was to enhance the culture and, since nurturing a culture requires constant awareness and reinforcement, their efforts had to be ongoing.

Members of all IMC's teams were told to let designated "culture checkers" know what was really happening—their concerns, feelings and the general condition of the hospital's team structure.

More formal checks took place at team meetings, starting from the time IMC's planners began their search for "perfect." These culture checks measured how things were working, with members of the team formally discussing the environment, examining the kind of feedback coming from members of other teams, physicians and patients. They looked at what was—and was not—working well with regard *Service Excellence*™.

This early attention to the basics of *Service Excellence*™ laid the groundwork for moving to the hospital, and inculcated the behaviors that later told patients, their families, physicians and even the team members that they were in a different environment.

Formal culture checks started with a series of questions designed to answer the basic concerns: "How is it going?" and "What is the attitude?"

Typical questions were:

• Are we preserving and protecting the culture?

• Are we helping maintain or reduce expenditures?

• Are we looking at ways to grow financially?

• Are we treating people—patients, families, physicians and each other—well?

• Are we cultivating the values and beliefs that we desire in our culture?

• Are we stimulating the expression of new ideas and looking for solutions to problems?

• Are we motivating team members to high levels of service creativity and performance and rewarding them for their effort?

• Are we working as a team?

The motto, Spirit of Service (S.O.S.*)*, became another tool for reinforcing the culture, evolving into a communication tool for reminding everyone of the ideal. S.O.S. stood for IMC's way of life, the way it did business and the basis for its *Service Excellence*™ culture. It was an attitude toward everyone, not just patients and physicians. It was based on how individuals treated each other as peers and members of the IMC team since, if it was not fully developed among team members, it could not be offered to the people IMC served.

Workers in health care have the special calling of serving patients, but their challenge differs from that facing people who serve customers in a restaurant, a department store or a gas station. Customers go to those businesses by choice and service burnishes their perception that they have received a worthwhile product or service for their money. By contrast, most people who come to a hospital would rather be anywhere else. They arrive nervous, apprehensive and, sometimes afraid. Thus, the responsibilities for *Service Excellence*™ in health care go well beyond the delivery of a specific product. They include easing the concerns patients have merely because they are in a hospital.

With this philosophical base, S.O.S. became a call to action, with which team members could signal others when they believed their actions might be moving away from the spirit. It also served as a quick signal of conflict between two team members with which one team member alerted the other that communication had broken down so each needed to pause and allow for more open dialogue. Thus, it helped keep the culture in line.

StethoScoop, IMC's lighthearted, friendly, slightly irreverent but still informational newsletter, was in keeping with IMC's sense of connectiveness. In addition to Brain Bowl information and stories on the things team members did for each other, it featured different hospital service areas and articles on what different professionals do, adding to the sense of understanding necessary to team camaraderie. In addition to articles contributed by IMC team members at all levels, *StethoScoop* included material derived from sources outside the hospital on the philosophy of service and on teams and team building.

To maintain a sense of accomplishment in its people, an organization must build in an appropriate mechanism to provide them with recognition. Ideally, this mechanism spreads the word about the positives of the system as well as about the special efforts of team members.

At IMC, if team members wanted to thank their peers for supporting IMC's Spirit of Service, they filled out Spirit Grams and sent them to IMC's president. He signed these public pats-on-the-back and passed them out, personally if possible, at all-team meetings or with a bit of pomp and circumstance at the recipient's workstation. Copies also went on Spirit Gram boards around the hospital for everyone to look at, and into the recipient's personnel file.

Another program, Walk in Your Shoes (WIYS), enforced the concept that all jobs were important. It underlined Shared Leadership and developed empathy by having colleagues do each other's jobs. WIYS required every team member to spend one day each calendar year handling someone else's work. In addition to providing an appreciation of the challenges in other jobs, the program symbolized how every job contributed to attaining *Service Excellence*™.

Pay-for-Performance System

IMC matched its Pay-for-Performance System to its goals to enforce both individual and team performance. Combining position descriptions, performance appraisal and compensation into a merit and bonus system gave everybody a piece of success. Each appraisal emphasized expectations, accountabilities and outcomes. It described the range of performance possible in a position and assessed an individual's performance in that position.

The merit and bonus system incorporated an ongoing review process that, in effect, made the review form a living document—a performance management contract for continuous improvement. In its ongoing form, there were midyear as well as traditional year-end reviews with an emphasis on team member development.

New team members received a specific position description and performance appraisal form when hired. Thus, they knew exactly what they were expected to do. Their first performance review came 90 days later. This meant there was a limited window for assuring that individual and corporate values were becoming aligned. The 90-day review led either to termination, if performance was unacceptable; to a formal performance improvement plan, if systematic development was needed; or to continuation of normal growth, if performance was acceptable. After that, the normal pattern of midyear and year-end reviews, based on a team member's starting date began. Thus someone was always due for review and everyone did not have to be considered in a time frame limited by arbitrary calendar dates.

The review criteria were broken into two basic parts: the technical aspects of the job and *Service Excellence*™. There were also segments dealing with cost effectiveness and professional growth (learning). Service excellence—the team component—accounted for half of each evaluation. Technical and functional competence in the team member's area of expertise accounted for 40 percent, with the other two segments counting for 5 percent each.

Evaluation forms provided a breakdown of the elements that made up these areas, many of which, particularly when it came service expectations, were far more qualitative than quantitative. The goal was for the highly subjective evaluation on the *Service Excellence*™ scale to be done, after appropriate organization-wide training, by each team member's peers. In the longer term, Peer Review was to become the heart of the evaluation process.

The system put a premium on service and attitude. The best surgical nurse in the world, from a technical point of view, was not expected to survive at IMC without being able to get along with other team members.

Learning to perform such reviews was one of the challenges of the system, since the descriptors were qualitative and nontraditional. The process involved both self-evaluation and an evaluator, who, initially, was a team leader or vice president. Individuals and evaluators each completed a form. The individuals sent their forms to the evaluators who compared the two and then they held a face-to-face performance review to ensure clear communication and understanding. Finally, all forms were signed and forwarded to Service Management.

The service criteria also looked at cooperation with the process, with teams and with team mates within the hospital's programs. Even within technical and functional competence, criteria reinforced cooperation and service, highlighting shared leadership, team participation, effective communication and initiative.

Salary increases were determined based on the annual review. A numerical evaluation was derived and determined merit raises. The amount received was linked to overall hospital performance according to percentages and the formula for increases was available to all team members.

Cross-Training and Other Learning Opportunities

IMC recognized that the experienced, high-powered professionals who made up its staff were very well educated but that hospital people in general, and clinical employees in particular, in traditional environments had not been allowed to use their educations. They had not been given the kind of responsibility and accountability they deserve and can handle.

IMC's training and education plans included developing comprehensive, excellent learning opportunities at all levels and for all groups, both within the hospital and outside in its community. Team members were told from their first job interview that everyone would be cross-trained. Indeed, IMC's long-term plan called for cross-training of all team members with the exception of some nurse specialist, by the end of the fourth year.

All job descriptions required between 10 and 40 percent of a team member's time to be set aside for administration. In some areas, team members periodically filled the role of facilitator to handle routine administrative functions and, in others, members volunteered for results-oriented work teams.

Facilitators were identified in areas that did not have team directors. They handled, on a rotating basis, functions performed by department heads in a traditional structure. Rotation gave everyone an opportunity to be in a leadership role and responsible for management aspects of their service area. This strengthened the team and enabled it to do more.

The nature of cross-training varied among service lines. For example, in Shared Services, team members with distribution and delivery functions did not handle food or medications exclusively. Someone who delivered medications one day might retrieve blood specimens the next. The goal was to enable team members to move freely between lab and pharmacy related responsibilities to cover spot vacancies.

Making cross-training pervasive reinforced the idea that "not my job" was an unacceptable statement.

IMC also developed learning opportunities for staff physicians, employees and patients and created ties to area schools, colleges and universities. Programs included:

- Accreditation for continuing medical education of staff physicians.

- *Service Excellence*™ training for team members and physicians.

- Community education.

- A unique form of health education for women.

- Development of a biomedical curriculum at Irvine Valley College.

- An educational advisory council.

Shared Leadership training was the basis of moving to self-managed work teams. Fundamental shared leadership training involved everyone and each session included a cross section of people, with vice presidents and associates working together. Participants sat at round tables and formed temporary teams to experience teamwork. People who didn't speak English sat with someone who interpreted for them, further reinforcing the need for cooperation. Some of the people took notes in another language and the training programs became an international experience but, regardless of language diversity, the standards of the training were high and teammates were expected to stretch themselves.

The training incorporated physical activities that allowed participants to cross international barriers. The activities required logical thinking rather than language skills so everyone could participate. People left these sessions with an immediate sense of total team. People who had never before felt included found themselves sitting next to a vice president or a team director or a college-educated professional, and their attitudes changed. There was a sharing hospitalwide, since literally everyone went through the "basic training."

Internal Communication

IMC developed internal communication systems and techniques for keeping everyone aware of organizational goals and activities. These were designed to reinforce the culture, to make sure everyone was apprised of and understood organizational priorities and to smooth the working of Shared Leadership and decision making at the point of service. Some of the devices for reinforcing communication, such as Spirit Grams and *StethoScoop,* are discussed above.

A uniform understanding of priorities is especially important when people are introduced to a vast number of projects at the same time. It must be clear which are primary and which are secondary. People must understand how these projects affect them and what their responsibilities are when they are involved.

One major potential pitfall of Shared Leadership is having individual decisions isolated from other team members. For example, hiring several skilled team members capable of making decisions about purchasing can lead to duplication of orders and excess inventory. The primary device used at IMC to combat this was the question: "Who else needs to know?" In the case of a patient care decision, the information went on the patient's care plan. In other cases, each time a person made a decision, it had to be put on a form headed with that question and transmitted in a timely manner to everyone else who might be affected. In the case of purchasing, for example, this included everyone on the team who might be called on to place a similar order.

Another facet of this communication was making sure that everyone involved in decisions received the information tracking their team's results. In this way, they—as a team—saw the consequences of their decisions and were able to adjust accordingly. If mistakes were made, they learned from them.

A second potential pitfall is a lack of control leading to things not getting done or to expense levels rising too high because nobody is "in charge." Overcoming this required cooperation among services, manifested in a ready exchange of information.

IMC's development curriculum established definite parameters within its four-years so that responsibility followed knowledge. Thus, self-scheduling was introduced in year one and budgeting in year two. These parameters said clearly that while everyone had the flexibility to make decisions, they first had to be trained.

Putting Financial Decisions and Information Downstream

To make decisions that are in the best interests of the organization requires financial information that is often unavailable at the lower levels of a traditional structure. Intelligent financial decisions require gathering up-to-the- minute data, which modern computer systems have made possible, and then applying common sense to the information.

IMC introduced team members to financial decision making, building their proficiency and fiscal accountability over the course of the four-year Shared Leadership development program. Everyone in the organization received monthly profit and loss statements for their teams and was expected to provide feedback and cost-effectiveness ideas based on their frontline expertise.

Team members had budgetary authority and the reports enabled them to spot quickly unexpected spending variance and facilitate hospital planning. Teams that overspent were asked to explain, since accountability goes with authority. With everyone aware of the financial needs and status of IMC, everyone was able to make better-informed decisions.

Quality Assurance—Feedback on Excellence

Quality assurance was the feedback mechanism that made sure IMC's *Service Excellence*™ goals were being met. It set service standards, checked to make sure they were being met and monitored customer satisfaction to verify that the goals were adequate. It answered the question, Do we do what we say we will do? If the answer was no, or if standards were being met and yet customers were not satisfied, then the system was adjusted.

IMC started planning its operations by looking at all aspects of the services it planned to offer and asked how they should be done: How should a patient be registered before entering the hospital? How should a patient be moved from one unit to another safely and with dignity? Who should be responsible for the patient's care?

Team members in each service area defined the important aspects of service that they provided and the expected patient outcomes. In line with the continuous improvement philosophies espoused by total quality management, these goals were constantly reevaluated.

For example, Imaging Services identified:

Aspect of Care (Behavior)	Expected Outcome (Standard)
1. Patient turn around time	• Patients shall wait no longer than 10 minutes for an X-ray.
2. Patient Saftey	• The Patient will not require repeat X-rays. • Patients will be assisted on and off exam tables.
3. Physician service	• Reports of X-ray results will be submitted to physicians on a timely basis.

In Emergency Services, a team goal was to serve patients within 60 seconds of their arrival. Only after assessing the urgency of patient's illness or injury and after stabilizing the condition would paperwork be completed. In addition, patients were welcome to have a friend or relative present during their emergency care. To maintain a positive relationship with both patients and physicians, the Emergency Services team worked with patient's personal physicians to ensure the continuity of their care. The team contacted the patient's primary physicians within 24 hours of the patient's visits to inform them of the patients' conditions and the care provided by IMC.

Employers whose employees required care experienced similar quality assurance. Workers' compensation patients were provided timely communication for their employers to minimize the paperwork confusion that can easily diminish the quality of service.

IMC developed a feedback mechanism to elicit, and listen to, the reactions of customers (the patients and physicians) and of members of other teams. Evaluation forms were distributed to patients, their families and physicians. The information received, both positive and negative, was fed back to the team(s) involved. A computer program allowed Service Management to keep track of the evaluations, watching for any patterns or diminishment of quality standards that might require intervention.

This process proved highly successful. Not only was there a great deal of positive feedback from IMC's community, but the accrediting board was favorably impressed.

Among the standards JCAHO sets for accreditation is one for quality assurance. It states as a criterion: "There is an ongoing quality assurance program designed to objectively and systematically monitor and evaluate the quality and appropriateness of patient care, pursue opportunities to improve patient care and resolve identified problems." After visiting IMC, a JCAHO team said IMC's Quality Assurance Program was one of the "best in the country."

External Communication

A hospital is big business and requires the same kind of external support in the way of advertising and public relations that make any big business grow, particularly in a highly competitive environment. For IMC, the service philosophy was an important marketing tool to be used formally, not just left to be spread by word of mouth.

What most physicians want from a hospital is happy patients and a minimum of hassle on their rounds. The good experiences patients had and their positive feedback to their doctors encouraged the physicians to increase their placement rates at IMC.

However, the endorsement that comes when people are talking about the "Wow! Knock your socks off" service must be publicized. Communications need to be geared to the various publics an organization serves. For a hospital, this begins, and in many cases, used to end with physicians. Acquainting them with its facilities is paramount, since encouraging them to bring in their patients provides the hospital's lifeblood. Marketing directly to patients has been of dubious value. Patients tend to go where their physicians send them, even in a changing health care environment that includes greater involvement of patients in decision making. Traditional views of promotional propriety also discourage such marketing.

IMC acknowledged the emphasis on physicians structurally by combining physician and marketing services, with the emphasis on physicians and by setting up its medical staff action teams. However, it relied heavily on the direct efforts of the president, largely through face-to-face meetings and speaking engagements, to promote IMC to this important public. To this, particularly when Shared Leadership is working effectively, must be added the presence in the community of vice presidents who run service lines and can promote IMC.

Building accredited lists of physicians was not a problem; getting them to actually *practice* at the hospital was. It cost physicians nothing to sign up and become credentialed while they were learning what IMC had to offer. It was a new hospital and they were going to cover their bases while continuing to practice where they had always practiced.

Private-practice physicians who had long wanted an Irvine community hospital and had pushed for its creation were the first to use it. Some took big risks to come to IMC after taking early stands to become visibly involved despite hostility from peers at other locations. IMC sought to keep these physicians involved, and to bring in additional physicians, using a version of Shared Leadership. Medical chiefs of services were selected by committees of physicians on the assumption that if physicians helped establish the services, they would use them.

Such involvement, in the highly competitive environment that existed, was a marked plus with young physicians starting out in private practice who could not penetrate entrenched physician bases at established hospitals and were interested in a new place where they were able to build business. The medical office building which was part of the IMC complex and was fully rented, was also a plus for the longer term in getting physicians involved.

Another plus, particularly for attracting physicians who already had healthy practices, was IMC's Physical Assessment and Reactivation (PAR) Center, a facility designed to support the Orthopædics Service. The PAR Center opened two years before the hospital and allowed doctors to send their patients for rehabilitation. By the time the hospital itself opened, established orthopædic surgeons were ready to admit their patients.

The PAR Center also served as a conduit to area business, offering industries an opportunity to assess the physical capacity of their employees. Using state-of-the-art equipment, this database helped reduce workers' compensation claims as well as lost work time.

IMC also effectively used traditional hospital marketing avenues such as providing meeting space, offering classes and special programs, and developing an active volunteer program, to involve the community.

Summary

• Identifying and involving people who share organizational values makes aligning the First and Second Orders less complicated. Clear, precise job profiles and behavioral assessment tools enhanced IMC's search process.

• Language reinforces the values of an organization, giving them a consistent presence in daily activities.

• Orientation programs at IMC, such as TEAM TIES, drew new people into the culture by creating involvement and long-term relationships.

• Acculturation was reinforced by ongoing activities which, took the form of action teams, suggestion programs, lunchtime meetings, recognition systems, skill-building retreats and other learning opportunities.

• Pay-for-performance was supported by a review process that emphasized an individual's adherence to IMC's values.

• IMC encouraged professional growth by designing a learning curriculum

• Effective communication requires that everyone who needs a piece of information receives it. Every decision at IMC was accompanied by the question Who else needs to know? Financial information, closely held in traditional hospitals, was made available to everyone since everyone was involved in decision making.

• Promoting a hospital in today's competitive environment requires the same kind of advertising and public relations as any other business.

Chapter 8. Third Order Change

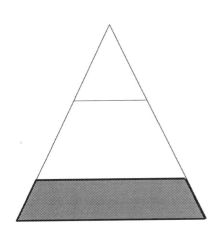

IMC developed detailed change and implementation plans to guide it to Third Order Change. Its change plan defined the fundamental changes desired, the framework for the organization and the articulation of the corporate values. Its implementation plan charted a strategy along with a timeline in which to achieve the change plan, including an ambitious ROI over a five-year period.

Another significant piece of the implementation plan was the four-year training curriculum. For each year, specific programs were identified that addressed both professional and behavioral training. Paramount was the belief that building a learning environment was the key to promoting the corporate values. Certain core programs were mandatory for everyone while others were based on particular needs. For example, *Service Excellence*™, team building and quality assurance were part of the core. Selective programs included specific on-the-job-training, technical skills and professional advancement. Hospital personnel normally limited to basic technical training found themselves in multidisciplinary sessions actively defining how to best meet patients' needs. The initial response was one of great skepticism that ideas from all parts of the hospital were valued; once ideas were implemented, that doubt was erased.

Individual Accountability

Each individual at IMC was accountable for every facet of the hospital's operation. A radical departure was requiring everyone to participate in the financial planning process. To start, everyone was expected to be able to read a budget. Efforts at IMC went beyond the perfunctory cost containment efforts of other hospitals. It believed that making fiscal accountability part of each individual would promote overall hospital efficiency. Understanding operating expenses and being held accountable for managing a budget was viewed as good business practice.

This was a significant paradigm shift. Secrecy surrounding budgets is not limited to hospitals. Sharing numbers with other than management is considered heretical. In most organizations, budgets and spending authority are indicators of power and authority, equated with control. At IMC, people with 20 years of hospital experience, when given the budget for their area to review, said they had never before seen a budget, much less been asked to give input to one.

Sharing of financial information at IMC was coupled with authority and accountability. Once negotiated and agreed upon, areas were expected to manage their budgets and were allowed spending authority. This was Third Order Change. It demonstrated going beyond the talk to walking the organizational values of individual trust, decision making at the point of service and shared responsibility.

Value Hiring

IMC engaged everyone in the hiring process, blasting apart another paradigm common to hospitals. Individuals applying to the hospital found themselves interviewed by cross-functional teams. To reinforce linkages with the total organization, these interviewers were selected from throughout the hospital. It was not unusual for people to find only one member of the service or area to which they were applying on the interview team. These interview teams were empowered to make final hiring decisions. They took the responsibility seriously. It was an opportunity to promote the organization's values to candidates as well as to demonstrate that IMC was indeed a different hospital. Sometimes, candidates were overwhelmed and opted to withdraw their applications, in itself proof that the process worked.

Values are at the core of an individual, difficult for one to articulate, impossible to assess. What is more often the case is that individuals are able to recognize if their values are skew to an organization. And the greater the disparity between an individual's values and the organization's values, the more discord there will be; eventually, either the individual, the organization or both will pay the price for the misalignment.

IMC's interview teams believed in what they were creating and they conveyed the corporate values to applicants. In the course of the interviews, they were able to discern whether a candidate fit into the IMC culture. Sometimes it was difficult for them to articulate their reservations but if they had the slightest hesitancy about a candidate, the rule of thumb was not to hire the individual.

Organizational Connectiveness

Inherent in Third Order Change is a systems approach manifested in the ability of the organization to integrate all of its subsystems (as defined in Part I). The connectiveness of all parts of the organization is complex. Organizations contain powerful subcultures. People tend to affiliate within their professions and occupations, their departments and units. These alliances sometimes are so strong that any effort to connect them meets with concerted resistance. Such homogenous groups grow up in traditional systems where their collective power can be used for the betterment of their members. At IMC, that collective power was unimportant. What was important was building and maintaining organizational connectiveness.

This departure from usual functional alliances was difficult for some people. They had associated with those they perceived as their peers, those who had similar educational experiences, who were licensed by the same agencies and whose career networks revolved around those associations. Working at IMC pushed them to rethink those paradigms. For example, the health care industry recognizes and celebrates Nurses Day. At IMC, a decision was made that recognition of one professional group was not in keeping with the team values. It instead proposed that a Team Day be celebrated.

Cutting across these alliances and bringing into alignment individuals with different points of view can be one of the most difficult challenges an organization faces when attempting to institutionalize Third Order Change. To succeed, it must continually stay focused on its stated values.

IMC took specific steps to minimize the formation of professional alliances. All action teams were multidisciplinary; ongoing culture checks and continuous improvements were part of doing business.

Communication Integrity

Another important indicator of Third Order Change is the integrity of an organization's communication . This is reflected in the comprehensive openness, honesty and fact-based information that is shared on a timely basis with everyone who needs to know. The effectiveness of communication is measured by the absence of any significant surprises, surprises that are indicative of miscommunication or communication after the fact.

IMC made communication integrity one of its performance measures. It set out a standard that individuals were accountable for disseminating accurate and timely information. The "Who Else Needs To Know" signs were posted throughout the hospital and on each person's desk as a continual reminder. Periodic surveys and informal interviews by culture teams were conducted to encourage people to identify any communication breakdowns along with recommended solutions.

Organizational Transformation

Third Order Change is transforming an organization from doing things differently to doing different things. It is revolutionary. It starts with a blank piece of paper, challenging the status quo, questioning every facet of the business. Most importantly, transformation deals with letting go. It challenges organizations to break with the past and create something new. It changes the essence of the organization.

Organizational transformation begins with a set of corporate values and developing ways to make those values a reality in the way the organization does business.

IMC began to build the *Hospital of the Future* by engaging its stakeholders in defining a set of desired organizational values. From the outset, IMC wanted its various constituencies to be active partners in creating the values, thus enhancing their active commitment to modeling those values in their daily work. The core team worked to create a vision of the way it wanted the hospital to be. Core team members developed a structure that reflected the organizational values with new forms of communication, empowerment with authority, Shared Leadership and teamwork. Externally, they set about to setting new industry standards for responsiveness to patient and physician needs.

By including everyone in the process, they were able to shift organizational workstyles, creating shared ownership in the success of the hospital as a total entity. They created an environment where their human resources became their best competitive advantage.

Since change is permanent and ongoing, when organizations reach Third Order Change they are embracing change as a way of life. These organizations are able to tolerate high levels of ambiguity, to actually seek out, cause change, and to more easily manage change.

IMC institutionalized change as a way to succeed in business. Individuals were encouraged to think outside the box, identify marketing opportunities and anticipate change. IMC's desire was to emerge as the market leader in the community while shaping the industry itself.

Summary

• Programs that cause revelations have a strong impact in cementing Third Order Change, shocking sceptics into accepting organizational values.

• At IMC, significant breaks with tradition that focused on system-wide participation included sharing budget figures, involving everyone in the hiring process, encouraging organizational connectiveness and enforcing communication integrity to draw everyone into supporting the culture.

• Third Order Change can occur only with the integration of the organization's subsystems.

Chapter 9. The *Hospital of the Future* Post-Mortem

The visionaries who designed and built IMC succeeded on many levels. They created a service organization that received glowing reviews from everyone who came in contact with it. They created a working environment that inspired not only extraordinary on-the-job performance but lifestyle changes as well. They created fundamental change based on organizational values.

However, because of external pressures that built up as the hospital dragged toward completion, the factors mitigating against its success grew. These included rising costs, the competitive environment and unrest at AMI.

Costs

The many delays in building IMC forced construction and operating costs higher, making it harder for the new facility to break even quickly and increasing tensions with the parent company.

When AMI sought a certificate of need to build IMC, the projected costs were $70 million. By the time IMC opened its doors ten years later, the costs had grown to $170 million, almost $1 million per bed. Some of the increased costs came from the growing lack of understanding at the parent company. For example, IMC designed its own internal computer system to track all of the elements of its interrelated culture. By the time IMC was nearing completion in 1988, still far short of its opening, AMI had entered into an agreement with another computer company to supply systems for all AMI hospitals. AMI mandated that IMC use this new system, which was designed for a traditional environment and therefore did not align with IMC's other subsystems. IMC had to cancel its own system and assume $5 million in costs as well as the added costs of installing the AMI system, which, by the time IMC opened, was ready for replacement.

Construction changes added to IMC's overall building costs. Some of these were external due to building codes and hospital regulatory agencies. After IMC opened, additional fiscal trouble developed because of mixed signals and failure to communicate purchases among several people responsible for ordering within the same area. Supplies are one of a hospital's major cost items. Traditionally, hospitals deal with a few suppliers who monopolize sales. Also, supplies are used as an enticement for physicians. The attitude is "We'll get you anything you want," so it becomes next to impossible to order generic medicines or supplies. Although IMC was determined not to be caught in this traditional trap, when forced to choose between a physician's desires and maintaining tight cost control, it yielded to the physician. The fear prevailed that the physician would go elsewhere.

Any organization that is held hostage by any stakeholder severely limits its own growth potential. The organization must strive to stay focused on its overall well-being and not yield to the whims of individuals. IMC's lesson in this regard added to its costs significantly.

Competition and External Communication

The delays heightened the competitive environment which, in 1986, had already led analyses to conclude the area was overbedded and to question the viability of a new facility. IMC's competitors had time to position themselves with neighborhood outpatient and clinic facilities to draw away IMC's natural patient base and to concentrate on the service areas they knew would be IMC's specialties. Some even began to adopt IMC's concepts, which they were in a better position to implement immediately.

IMC was not prepared for battle. It had correctly recognized that to be successful, it had to offer something above and beyond what other facilities were offering, and it had recognized that this something extra would be *Service Excellence*™, since cutting-edge technology, eventually, is available to everybody. While IMC may have created the best of all possible internal worlds, that did not guarantee success. A unique culture has no business value until it is demonstrated, and the one area where IMC did not face and foster change was in its promotional activities.

For years, hospitals had considered active competition and orchestrated advertising and public relations activities unprofessional and inappropriate. By the late 1980s, this was changing and the support of the community leaders who had spearheaded IMC's construction was not in itself enough to attract people who were already being treated at traditional facilities in the area and had no compelling reason to move. Despite this, IMC continued to ignore or downplay, in any formal sense, the topic of competition.

In some ways, IMC was invisible. For its first year, it did not have a sign that was seen unless people were in front of the building. Plans for signage visible from a distance had been made from the beginning but, despite this lead time and the strong community support, they were stymied by pressure brought by competitors on the city to delay permission to erect the signage.

IMC's formal public relations and marketing efforts were forced to match those of AMI. Material distributed was generally informative in nature, stating that the hospital was open, nearby and convenient, without addressing the culture. Glowing articles about IMC appeared in the professional press, but the developments they lauded were not promoted in the general press where the public could read it. Initial marketing efforts were by direct mail and through ads in local papers, but the ads did not differentiate IMC from its competition. Structurally, many of the ads were ineffective at building awareness of IMC. The Irvine Medical Center name appeared in small print at the bottom of statements that emphasized, in isolation, a service line, thus failing to build a continuity of awareness of a hospital with a full range of services. Given AMI's distaste for "hard" sell, IMC was unable to take advantage of public relations opportunities.

AMI's Impatience

At AMI itself, over the years of delays, there had been five changes in leadership and ownership. With each corporate change, IMC's growing costs were viewed as a greater liability. The original corporate visionaries who had fostered the project were long gone and by 1990 no one at AMI wanted to be identified with IMC. The concept of IMC as a testing ground for precedent-setting ideas to benefit all AMI hospitals was lost in closed corporate files and departed memories.

With no advocate within AMI, IMC became alienated from its parent. People at IMC who had been part of AMI for years found it very hard to be ostracized by the whole organization. At corporate meetings, "Irvine bashing" became the thing to do and representatives of IMC were isolated.

The degree of misunderstanding was demonstrated when one of AMI's chief financial officers visited IMC, went back to headquarters and announced,"They have a cult down there." The comment arose because the CFO didn't know where registration fell in the organization structure since it wasn't part of finance. No one at AMI understood the structure and no one took the time to understand it. All they knew was that it didn't fit every other AMI hospital and half of the corporation's total capital expenditures budget was being sent to IMC. Therefore, something was wrong.

The reaction of the members of IMC's core team only made matters worse. The more IMC was criticized, the more they withdrew. Instead of attempting to educate the executives who had replaced their advocates, they circled their wagons, allowing the rift to grow.

In February 1990, with a June 1990 expected opening (pending final licenses and permits), IMC's core team hired, in a rush, the 450 individuals who would put IMC to work. In May, they began the task of integrating them into a team and watched as additional delays, this time related largely to a shortage of government inspectors, again pushed the opening back.

For instance, Orange County, at that time the fastest growing industrial area in the country, only had one fire inspector, who could allot only three hours a week to a job that was estimated to take four weeks to complete working full time.

Enforced idleness took a toll on the morale of those hired. Then a slow start to admissions after the hospital finally opened on August 5, 1990, led to staff shrinkage and added to the stress. Individuals became disillusioned; some left.

At AMI, the massive capital expenses dominated thinking. Despite the fact that a start-up operation requires an estimated three to five years from the day its doors open to eliminate its capital debt, AMI executives were demanding that IMC eliminate its debt in eighteen months. Under the best of circumstances, this was unrealistic, ignoring a number of industry dynamics, not the least of which was the conservative nature of physicians. Although 800 requested staff privileges, that did not guarantee even half would begin practice at IMC from day one. IMC had to prove itself. Physicians had to be convinced to use IMC rather than longer established hospitals in the area.

Still, the number of physicians recruited was a good sign. Projections in the evaluations done in 1986 indicated that up to 230 physicians needed to be recruited and refer half of their admissions to IMC to provide the occupancy needed to approach break even; with 800 accredited, each would have to refer fewer than 15% of their admissions to IMC for it to succeed.

Initially, physician conservatism limited the number of patients who experienced IMC's quality service. Occupancy for the first year lagged well behind an overly optimistic set of projections that grew strictly from a corporate need to justify the extremely ambitious and expensive facility. By AMI's calculations, IMC initially hemorrhaged money at a rate of $5 million a month but, compared with IMC's more realistic projections, it was on target.

Creating another huge road block, the new owner of AMI decided to make IMC a Real Estate Investment Trust (REIT) so the property could be carried on its books making money from rent separately from hospital operations. Thus, in addition to trying to reduce its debt, the hospital was faced with high rent.

As IMC made its mark, its growth accelerated. With the praise of its operations in the medical press and by the JCAHO, provider contracts and managed care plans that had been waiting for it to be accredited were put in place. This attracted additional doctors. Patient census grew and, based in the dedication of its gifted staff and the care orientation of its value driven culture, the IMC differences finally began to spell success.

The hospital began hitting its projected targets by February, 1992, eighteen months after it opened, a very reasonable time lag. This was especially true given its size and its highly competitive service area. AMI had facilities that had been running for as many as five years before they met their budgets. Yet IMC's performance was not perceived as good enough and, as had been done in East Cooper and West Alabama, AMI pulled the plug on the *Hospital of the Future*.

In its impatience, AMI gradually replaced the visionaries who designed the hospital with traditionalists whose eyes focused on the bottom line and who did not understand how IMC differed from the norm and what the differences meant. It was a classic example of what occurs when there is no long-term commitment at the top of the organization. Only the short-term problems are seen. Long-term opportunities and the potential for a better future are discounted. Traditional practices, encouraged by corporate leaders who were never involved in the vision, prevailed and IMC is now just another hospital. The professionals who saw what was possible and were not prepared to settle for less took their dreams and left.

Lessons Learned

Though the *Hospital of the Future* is no longer, many lessons were learned, not the least of which are the pitfalls of standing alone in a traditional world. The need for dedication and stable, committed leadership is mandatory in implementing fundamental change.

IMC reinforced the lessons learned in the United Kingdom. The hospitals there successfully achieved Third Order Change and a culture that made them highly profitable. Every Executive Director in the UK operation institutionalized fundamental change and exhibited leadership that supported the change. Everyone owned the process and made it *the* way to do business. This provided both commitment from the top and time for implementation. For IMC, pressures from outside the system—both from being a start-up facility and from its corporate parent—meant time would run out. Four-year programs are fine only when there are four years in which to implement them.

A culture like IMC's is pervasive and demanding. The culture permeated the lives of the believers, it changed lives, it influenced values. Those who developed IMC learned that their ideas worked. IMC was more than just a hospital. It was a revolution, challenging everything about health care delivery. It was an answer to the changing and competitive environment surrounding today's—and tomorrow's—hospital. It was about caring and managing change before it happens. It was a movement that concentrated on living organizational values with patients, their families, physicians, caregivers and the community as a whole. It was a breeding ground for individual and team accountability. It was change in action—managing by values.

The creation of IMC brought together theory, practice and external reality. Each of these facets hold lessons for the future of health care in particular and business organizations in general.

Everyone at IMC believed in its success. Team members saw in it the direction that health care delivery must take if health care is to meet the future needs of patients. Their conviction was not daunted even when an unbending corporate hierarchy pushed the hospital's structure back to the past. Change in the way health care is delivered must still come. Whoever gets there first will lead the industry into the next century.

Summary

• The elements that made up the *Hospital of the Future* proved effective but the whole failed under pressure from outside the system. Rising costs, competitive pressures and, the disappearance of advocates within the parent corporation destroyed the ability of its management team to carry out its implementation plan. The project, in counterpoint to the change process in the United Kingdom, proved the basic premise that Third Order Change requires commitment from the top.

• The hospital that engages in organizational transformation will shape the future of health care.

NOTES

[1] Peter B. Vaill, *Managing as a Performing Art* (San Francisco, CA: Jossey–Bass Publishers, 1989), p.2.

[2] Stan Davis, *Managing Corporate Culture* (Cambridge, MA: Ballinger Publishing Company, 1984), p.1.

[3] Morris Massey, (video) *What You Are Is What You Were When* (Schaumburg, IL: Video Publishing House, Inc.).

[4] Marvin R. Weisbord, *Organizational Diagnosis* (Reading, MA: Addison–Wesley Publishing Co., 1978), p.9.

[5] Peter Senge, *The Fifth Discipline: The Art and Practice of the Learning Organization* (New York, NY: Doubleday/Currency, 1990), p.251.

[6] *Success Magazine,* May, 1991.

[7] Senge, p.140.

[8] Vaill, p.2.

[9] Peter F. Drucker, *The New Realities* (New York, NY: Harper & Row Publishers, 1989), p.179.

BIBLIOGRAPHY

Argyris, Chris. *Knowledge for Action: A Guide to Overcoming Barriers to Organizational Change.* San Francisco: Jossey-Bass Publishers, 1993.

Beckhard, Richard and Pritchard, Wendy. *Changing the Essence: The Art of Creating and Leading Fundamental Change in Organizations.* San Francisco: Jossey-Bass Publishers, 1991.

Belasco, James A., Ph.D. *Teaching the Elephant to Dance: Empowering Change in Your Organization.* New York: Crown Publishers, Inc., 1990.

Bennis, Walter and Nanus, Burt. *Leaders: The Strategies for Taking Charge.* New York: Harper and Row, 1985.

Block, Peter. *The Empowered Manager: Positive Political Skills at Work.* San Francisco: Jossey-Bass Publishers, 1987.

ibid. *Stewardship: Choosing Service Over Self-Interest.* San Francisco: Berrett–Koehler Publishers, 1993.

Davis, Stanley M. *Managing Corporate Culture.* Cambridge, MA: Ballinger Publishing Company, 1984.

Drucker. Peter F. *The New Realities.* New York, NY: Harper & Row Publishers, 1989.

Galbraith, Jay R.; Lawler, Edward E. and Associates. *Organizing for the Future: The New Logic for Managing Complex Organizations.* San Francisco: Jossey-Bass Publishers, 1993.

Hamel, Gary and Prahalad, C.K. *Competing for the Future: Breakthrough Strategies for Seizing Control of Your Industry and Creating the Markets of Tomorrow.* Boston: Harvard Business School Press, 1994.

Handy, Charles. *The Age of Unreason.* Boston: Harvard Business School Press, 1989.

Kanter, Rosabeth Moss. *When Giants Learn to Dance: Mastering the Challenges of Strategy, Management and Careers in the 1990s.* New York: Simon and Schuster, 1989.

Katzenbach, Jon R. and Smith, Douglas K. *The Wisdom of Teams: Creating the High-Performance Organization* Boston: Harvard Business School Press, 1993.

Kennedy, Rose L. and Fisher, Linda R. *Traveling Through White Water: A Manager's Guide for Organizational Change.* Northbrook, IL : KF Enterprises, Inc. 1989.

Kilmann, Ralph H. *Beyond the Quick Fix: Managing Five Tracks to Organizational Success.* San Francisco: Jossey-Bass Publishers, 1984.

Laborde, Genie Z. *Influencing with Integrity: Management Skills for Communication and Negotiation.* Palo Alto, CA: Syntony Publishing, 1983.

Land, George and Jarman, Beth. *Breakpoint and Beyond.* Harper Business, 1992.

Lawler, Edward E., III. *The Ultimate Advantage: Creating the High-Involvement Organization.* San Francisco: Jossey-Bass Publishers, 1992.

Massey, Morris. (Video) *What You Are Is What You Were When.* Schaumburg, IL: Video Publishing House, Inc.

Mink, Oscar G; Mink, Barbara P.; Downes, Elizabeth A. and Owen, Keith Q. *Open Organizations: A Model for Effectiveness, Renewal and Intelligent Change.* San Francisco: Jossey-Bass Publishers, 1994.

Nadler, Gerald and Hibino, Shozo. *Breakthrough Thinking: Why We Must Change the Way We Solve Problems and the Seven Principles to Achieve This.* Rocklin, CA: Prima Publishing and Communications, 1990.

Nanus, Burt. *Visionary Leadership.* San Francisco: Jossey-Bass Publishers, 1992.

Peters, Tom. *Thriving on Chaos: Handbook for a Management Revolution.* New York: Alfred A. Knopf, 1987.

Rogers, David J. *Waging Business Warfare: Lessons from the Military Masters in Achieving Corporate Superiority.* New York: Charles Scribner's Sons, 1987.

Schaef, Ann Wilson and Fassel, Diane. *The Addictive Organization.* San Francisco: Harper and Row Publishers, 1988.

Schein, Edgar H. *Organizational Culture and Leadership.* San Francisco: Jossey-Bass Publishers, 1985.

Senge, Peter M. *The Fifth Discipline: The Art & Practice of the Learning Organization.* New York: Doubleday Currency, 1990.

Tichy, Noel M. and Sherman, Stratford. *Control Your Destiny or Someone Else Will: Lessons in Mastering Change—the Principles Jack Welch is Using to Revolutionize General Electric.* New York: Harper Collins Publishers, 1993.

Tichy, Noel M. and Devanna, Mary Anne. *The Transformational Leader.* New York: John Wiley and Sons, 1986.

Vaill, Peter B. *Managing as a Performing Art.* San Francisco, CA: Jossey–Bass Publishers, 1989.

Weisbord, Marvin R. *Organizational Diagnosis: A Workbook of Theory and Practice.* Reading, MA: Addison-Wesley Publishing Company, 1978.

ibid. *Productive Workplaces: Organizing and Managing for Dignity, Meaning and Community.* San Francisco: Jossey-Bass Publishers, 1991.

Wheatley, Margaret J. *Leadership and the New Science: Learning about Organization from an Orderly Universe.* San Francisco: Berrett-Koehler Publishers, 1992.